W9-AOJ-222

GAMES FOR GROWING CHILDREN:

AN ILLUSTRATED GUIDE
FOR TEACHERS AND PARENTS

by

Marian Jenks Wirth

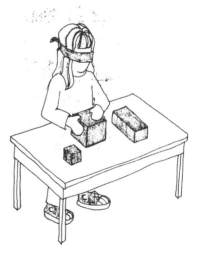

Illustrations by *Carol Damhorst*

Parker Publishing Company, Inc.   West Nyack, New York

> *To Art, Vicki, Scott and Patty*
> *and to the staff and children of*
> *The Miriam School*
> *who gave me support and many game ideas.*

© 1976 *by*

Parker Publishing Company, Inc.
West Nyack, New York

Originally published as

*Teacher's Handbook of Children's Games:
A Guide to Developing Perceptual-Motor Skills*

P.E.P. Books Edition . . . . . March 1981

Library of Congress Cataloging in Publication Data

Wirth, Marian Jenks,
   Teacher's handbook of children's games.

   Bibliography: p.
   Includes index.
   1. Educational games--Handbooks, manuals, etc.
2. Perceptual motor learning--Handbooks, manuals,
etc. I. Title.
LB1029.G3W54   372.1'3   76-12417

Printed in the United States of America

Foreword

This is a resource book that gives both the "why" and the "what" of developmental teaching of visual-motor skills. All who are involved in learning situations with elementary children will find the contents of this volume of great practical import. The "new look" in individualizing teaching necessitates a basic understanding of what it means to teach developmentally, with full recognition of the importance of including activities that enhance both fine and gross motor skills. The wide range of games and exercises in this book makes available to the reader a full repertoire of activities that are directed toward the achievement of specific developmental goals, clearly set forth and described by the author.

For too long, at the elementary level, the teaching of motor skills has been left to the physical education teacher, who generally has placed much emphasis on gamesmanship and competition. Youngsters who are "turned on" by phys-ed are usually those who are well developed motorically, headed toward being athletic during the school years. Those who are "turned off" and seek to avoid physical education are children with poorly developed motor skills. Developmental teaching of motor skills, by classroom teachers as well as by phys-ed teachers, makes it possible for all children to participate, enjoy and benefit in many ways from the experience.

In contrast to elementary teachers, kindergarten teachers have had a heritage of teaching both fine and gross motor skills to all young students. Within recent years, however, there has been an increasing tendency for many teachers to de-emphasize the teaching of motor-readiness skills due to the push to teach formal reading at an early age. This is most unfortunate and fails to give credence to knowledge gained from past research which indicates that bright children who learn to read at an early age do not read and comprehend as well as equally bright children who learn to read at a later age, when readiness skills are more fully developed.

Teachers of young children who fail to recognize the vital need for teaching visual-motor skills, both gross and fine, on a developmental basis, overlook the importance of the relationship of such developmental skills to the following aspects of learning in general: 1) the development of the ability to attend and concentrate; 2) the development of the ability to coordinate eye and hand in carrying out all of the many workbook and writing activities in school; 3) the development of thinking skills that are dependent on the integration of visual-motor skills, leading to high-level language comprehension.

The reader will become aware rapidly of how thoughtfully and well put together this resource book is. It is not just another compendium of motor tasks. Marian Wirth has gathered these experiences through her many years as Perceptual-Motor Teacher at the Miriam School with special children, young children of normal intellectual potential who have severe emotional and/or learning disorders. Among these youngsters have been many with major perceptual disabilities and very limited attention spans. These special children have come to enjoy doing these tasks when presented developmentally. It is assured that *all* children will enjoy and benefit from participating in such tasks during recess, free time, or specified classroom times. These well-organized activities will enable a teacher to feel free and comfortable in making visual-motor work an integral part of the school curriculum.

Eleanore T. Kenney, Ph.D.
Director,
The Miriam School

The Importance of Perceptual-Motor Skills

This is a practical handbook for all those who teach young children. Each chapter will help you to stimulate and contribute to the intellectual growth of the young child through the use of active physical games. Of course, the games will benefit the child's physical health and emotional well-being too. However, the primary goal of this book is to provide experiences and the type of real-life, active encounters upon which higher learning (conceptual or symbolic learning) is based.

A large part of the young child's day is spent gathering information from countless learning experiences involving movement and sensory stimulation. Gradually this information is sorted into key categories without which academic or school learning cannot take place. If all has gone well with the young child, we say he or she comes to school with readiness skills. He or she is ready to learn—this means he or she is now ready to learn symbols and complex concepts.

However, readiness to learn is itself a collection of learned knowledge. It *can* be taught, and should not be left to chance.

Let's look at an example of how a very young child learns through movement and sensory stimulation. Let's say a toddler, sitting on his kitchen floor is handed a new terry-cloth toy dog. He turns it around and around in his hands, strokes it against his face, and tastes the fuzzy surface, all the while looking at the toy dog from every angle. He feels *while seeing*, its size, shape, and weight, squeezes its rubber stuffing, perhaps hears a little squeak inside. He looks at and feels the legs, the button eyes, the red felt tongue, and the stiff string whiskers. Perhaps his parents say "doggie" repeatedly. During all of this experience he is matching visual, tactual, and auditory information with the kinesthetic "feel" of the toy as it turns in his hands, is held up in the air, is dropped and picked up, or squeezed against his body. This is an elementary example of perceptual-motor learning.

The next time our child sees another type of toy dog, or another type of terry-cloth toy, or perhaps a real dog, he will bring to the new experience some already-learned information from his information "bank." Still later, after many more similar experiences, he will be able to see a *picture* of a dog or toy dog, and be able to connect meaning to it. And much later, when he sees the word symbol "dog," he will be able to call up a whole file of information based on dozens or hundreds of separate, seemingly insignificant experiences centered around dogs. He now has a *concept* that he can use in his thinking in many different ways.

The Benefits of Perceptual-Motor Games

1. *Intellectual*—First, these games provide the child with lots of interesting, first-hand information about the physics of the surrounding environment:

concepts of size, shape, color, weight;

concepts of time and space, distance and speed (including fast and slow, now, and then, later; first, second, third; here, there, etc.)

the knowledge and language of place and position: over, under, around, beside, in front of, behind, between, in, on, etc.

number concepts, and the beginnings of visual symbols. (Visual marks that indicate a place to wait, to move across, or signal some action or response to be made, all constitute a primitive form of reading.)

2. *Physical Benefits*—Perceptual-motor games enable the child to develop a body that is working at peak efficiency—a body that can move when, where, and how the situation requires; a body that will not tire easily; a body whose sensory organs are working with efficiency and depth and which are able to give accurate and relevant information to the brain.

Through games, the automatic control of the body is gradually given over to a competent leader or boss: the child's own brain. In learning to subdue impulse, the child acquires true freedom.

3. *Psychological Benefits*—Third, physiological readiness games give a child confidence in himself as an independent person, self-aware and autonomous. After having solved the myriad concrete problems involved in games (and all games are in a sense puzzles), he acquires increased certainty of his problem-solving abilities. He also has acquired the skills of organizing the sequence of steps needed to solve a problem: visualizing the problem, formulating a plan, moving through the plan making connections and corrections on the way, and thus resolving the problem.

Additional benefits of the perceptual-motor games to be found in this book:

Right and left awareness, directions sense.

Visual skills: tracking, focus, steering the hands and body.

A basis for fine motor coordination.

Social skills: game know-how, taking turns, sharing, toleration of minor frustration.

Listening, concentrating, increasing attention span, auditory discrimination.

Memory: short and long term; auditory and visual.

Pacing, transition (from fast to slow, from intense attention to scanning, etc.).

Impulse control, quick reactions, stop and start, anti-perseveration.

Thinking while doing, coordinating mind and body.

Creativity, improvisation, enjoyment.
Large and small space judgment (visual discrimination).
Vocabulary, speech and language development.

Perceptual-motor games will enable you to help a child extend his attention span, feel better about himself and his body, increase his ability to get along with his peers, and increase his language skills. They can indeed result in a learning bonanza. They have contributed dramatically to improved learning in the classroom in which I teach perceptual-motor skills . . . and I'm certain they can do the same for you. Perceptual-motor game time may well become the most learning-productive part of your childrens' school day.

Marian Jenks Wirth

Table of Contents

11

1.

Balance

A child's balance is intimately related to his self-awareness and self-confidence. Experience with gravity is one of the infant's earliest lessons; a sense of the center of self is necessary for understanding space and judging distance. And out of the sense of space and distance arise concepts of time, direction, left and right.

1. / Balance Add-Ons

The game develops:

> Balance and coordination.
> Memory.
> Sense of the sequence of events (organization).
> Creativity.

Age: Children age four can do three or four add-ons. Older children can do up to six or seven, perhaps more.

Materials: A rope or string seven feet long for each child is helpful but not necessary.

Directions:

Child #1 makes a rope circle on the floor, steps in, and does a simple balancing stunt, such as standing on the left foot. He steps out, leaving the rope circle on the floor.

Child #2 steps in the first rope circle, stands on the left foot. She then adds

Balance Add-Ons

on a new rope circle touching the first, steps into it and does a new balance stunt, for example, balances on tiptoes with eyes shut.

Child #3 steps into the first circle and repeats balance stunt #1; steps into second circle and repeats balance stunt #2. If he remembers to do these correctly, he adds on another rope circle, and executes stunt #3. This might be balancing on the right foot and the left knee. If he does *not* do the first two stunts correctly, he is not allowed to add on.

Variations: The game may be played in small groups, with each child having two turns.

Comments: If the child cannot think up a simple stunt, the teacher may whisper one in his or her ear.

Children who can never seem to remember three verbal commands in a row (such as, go to your locker, get your coat, and bring it back), may remember four or five or more stunts in a row—partly because there is visual demonstration, partly because the game is low-key and fun.

Other balance stunts might include:

a) Balance on one foot, one knee and one elbow,
b) Balance on two feet and the head, etc.,
c) Balance on two feet and one hand,
d) Balance sitting, feet just off floor.

2. / Tin-Can Stilts

For:

Balance.
Laterality: coordination of left and right sides of body.
Finger, hand, and arm strength.

Age: All ages. Even age four's can work small stilts made out of low, wide (coffee) cans. Older children can work taller stilts made out of tall juice cans.

Materials: Several pairs of stilts made out of two (large juice or other) cans with the bottoms cut out; punctured at the top with a beverage can opener (two holes on opposite edges of top); and each can tied with a rope looped through the holes and tied with a large knot inside the can. Ropes should be hip high.

If the can has a plastic cover (such as a coffee can) you may replace the cover on the bottom of the stilts for slip resistance. However, I think the click of metal on a tile floor has a nice horsey sound.

Directions: The secret to making the stilts work is to pull up hard on the ropes

Tin-Can Stilts

as you walk. The child may walk around the edge of the room, between or over tape lines, backwards, forwards or sideways. He or she can sound like a prancing horse, or have a relay race with several teams participating.

Comments: Start small children by walking peg-leg style with only one stilt. Some children seem to get the stilts on easier by sitting in a chair, some by standing.

Children who tumble off the stilts never seem to hurt themselves. Perhaps it's because when using the stilts, they are in a somewhat curled position. Teach children to fall down "like an old coat slipping off a hook."

It is better to practice indoors where the floor is smooth. A rug is slightly harder to walk on but the falls are soft. A thick rug makes walking too difficult. A stronger set of stilts may be made by *not* cutting the bottom out of the can. It's harder to wiggle the rope through the punctured holes, but it can be done.

3. / Balance Beam Pick-A-Card

For:

> Balance, coordination, various locomotor patterns.
> Body awareness in various positions.
> Integrating verbal directions, visual demonstration, and motor actions.
> Language of body parts, positions, direction, space.
> Memory sequential and/or immediate.
> Making transitions and changes; attention span increase.

Age: All ages. The game is best done in groups of about four to six children to avoid long waits for a turn.

Materials: A balance beam. A 2″ × 2″ × 8′, or a 2″ × 4″ × 8′ board would do. A set of eight or ten (or more) cards, with a simple balance stunt typed on each. (See below.)

Directions: Children sit in a row against the wall. One by one, they go to the pile of face-down cards, pick one, and read it or have it read to them. The card then goes into a "done" pile. The child steps up onto the beam, does his or her stunt, and steps off the beam. The child then returns to the end of the line by any special method, for example, the crab-walk.

Child #2 picks a new card, does the stunt as directed, and returns to the end of the line crab-style.

Balance Beam Pick-A-Card

Variations:
1. *All* children repeat the stunt which the first child demonstrated. (All children follow child #1 across, etc. Each child does all stunts.)
2. For language practice, have each child describe in words just what he or she did on the beam. Give assistance as needed.

Examples of stunts:
Go across beam carrying bean bag on head.

Go to center, turn around once, continue to end of beam.

Go across beam with giant steps.

Go across beam while tossing beanbag in air.

Go across beam, stop at center and toss bean bag into a box.

Walk beam with eyes closed.

Walk sideways, left foot leading.

Invent a new way to cross.

Comments: Even very wiggly children, who ordinarily have trouble waiting for a turn, are raptly attentive during this game.

Children like to pick their own written direction cards, even when they cannot read, in preference to being *told* what to do by the teacher.

While in general it is always preferable that children *not* wait long periods for a turn, there is benefit in watching these stunts as well as doing them.

4. / Blind Persons' Carnival

For:

> Balance, agility, and body awareness using simple equipment.
> Mental planning, describing in words, and execution of an original idea.

Age: All ages. Older children may be expected to give more detail, and execute more complex actions.

Materials: Any simple equipment. Two boards with three trestles are ideal. (See Improvised Obstacle Course, p. 134.) Dark glasses for the teacher to wear are helpful but not necessary.

Directions: Set up one or two stations, for example, station #1 might be a wide eight foot board with one end raised on a trestle as a slide. Station #2 might be another board arranged as a bridge between two trestles.

Tell the children the following story: "Pretend you are going to a carnival." (Discuss carnival.) "Pretend that I (the teacher) and my friend (an aide or an older child) own the carnival, and we are blind. These dark glasses mean we can't see." (The teacher may close eyes from time to time instead.)

"We like to have children come to our carnival, but you must do some work to earn permission to use the 'rides.' Here is what you have to do: Since we (the ladies or men who own the carnival) are blind, we require each of you to say what you plan to do on the bridge or the slide. If you tell us what you will do, you will be allowed to use our carnival toys (rides). You might say,'I'm going to jump down the slide,' or you might say, 'I'm going to slide down on my back, head first.' When you get to the bridge, you might say, 'I'm going to hop halfway across, and then jump as far as I can.' " Young children may use simpler ideas and simpler words.

Comments: By requiring children to plan a simple stunt before they do it, you are helping them learn to plan and predict, organize themselves mentally and set up a simple sequence. They must translate ideas into verbal symbols. They must then mobilize the physical actions needed to carry out the plan. These are by no means easy skills, and much help should be given the child who is having difficulty thinking up a stunt, or putting it into words. Any and all efforts should be praised. Children should be allowed to copy each other if necessary.

Blind Persons' Carnival

In practice, children are highly motivated by the game and with little or no stress, will be able to plan, verbalize, and execute a simple stunt with relative ease. The skills involved are extremely useful in what we call "learning to think."

2.

Blindfold Games

There is no better way to develop the hearing or touching senses than through blindfold games. Many children rely heavily, sometimes too heavily on sight. Yet a great deal of academic and other information must come from the hearing sense. All senses should be as fully developed as possible so that the child can function on all sense "cylinders."

5. / Sometimes I'm Tall

The game develops:

> Hearing sense (localizing sounds).
> Social skills: taking turns and remembering who has or has not had a turn.
> Body awareness in tall or small positions.

Age: Young children primarily.

Materials: None. A blindfold (bandana or scarf) is helpful but not necessary.

Directions: Children stand in a circle except for "It," who is blindfolded and standing with his back to the group. Children in circle say:
> "I'm very, very tall (stretch arms up, stand on tiptoe)
> I'm very, very small (stoop down, fold self into ball)
> Sometimes I'm tall (stretch up again)

Sometimes I'm Tall

Sometimes I'm small (fold up)."
  (Pause. Teacher or leader indicates with a hand signal whether the
    group is to be tall or small, just before the last line is spoken.)
"Guess what we are now."
  Blindfolded child tries to figure out from the "height" of the voices whether
the group is tall or small. Whether or not he guesses correctly, the turn passes.
Whoever is "It" may pick the next "It."

Variation: In the tall position, children speak loudly. In the small position, they
speak softly.

Comments: Tell children at the beginning that it's hard to tell if the group is
tall or small, that it doesn't matter whether or not they guess correctly, and that
the guessing is mostly for fun.

6. / Who Is Knocking At My Door?

For:

Learning to identify sounds.
Memory ("What makes that sound?").
Extending attention span: listening for signals and sounds.

Taking turns and following simple rules.
Holding self immobile and silent, yet relaxed.

Age: All ages. Some young children may need help getting used to wearing a blindfold.

Who Is Knocking At My Door?

Materials: A blindfold (bandana or scarf) and a chair.

Directions: Children sit in a semicircle except for "It" who sits in a chair, with her back to the children, blindfolded. The teacher points to another child, who goes up to the chair, kneels down and knocks on it.

"It" asks, "Who is knocking at my door?"

The kneeler answers, disguising his voice, saying, "It's me" or answers by barking, meowing, crowing, etc.

"It" tries to guess who the kneeler is. If she guesses correctly, the turn passes to someone, usually to the kneeler, who has not had a turn.

If "It" cannot guess correctly, the kneeler knocks again and repeats the process. If, after three tries, "It" still cannot guess, the turn passes.

Variation: Play "*What* is knocking at my door?" The kneeler puts a common object into the hands of "It," who tries to identify it (spoon, pencil, chalk, etc.). See also Localizing Sounds, p. 166.

Comments: This is a good game for winding down after a period of active play. The wiggliest child will sit still for it, and the game never seems to get stale. If a child is uncomfortable wearing a blindfold, it helps to let him or her watch other children wearing one.

7. / Marco Polo

For:

Increasing auditory and tactile awareness.
Body awareness: guiding the body without visual cues.
Social give and take, and game strategy.

Age: Young children may play the game in a relatively small circle; older children may play a faster and more difficult game in a larger space. The teacher may adjust the circle size to class needs and abilities, so that "It" can find his partner within about one minute.

Materials: A bandana, or other blindfold. A long rope that defines the boundary of the circle is very helpful, but not necessary.

Marco Polo

Directions: Children form a circle, and hold a long circular rope. This forms a boundary for the blindfolded child to bump against if need be. Circle children *could* use outstretched arms to indicate where the edge of the circle is.

Two children stand inside the circle. Child #1 is blindfolded. She is the chaser and is called Marco. Child #2 is the runner; he is Polo. From time to time Marco calls her name, "Marco!" She may call as often as she wishes. Every time Child #1 calls "Marco," Child #2 *must* answer "Polo." The calls and answers enable Child #1 to locate Child #2 and tag him. When the chaser is caught, roles may be reversed, or two other children may take turns in the center. The runner and chaser should be helped to learn the strategies of their roles: the runner will learn to answer "Polo" and quickly duck away to the other side of the circle. The chaser, Marco, will learn she will catch Polo more easily if she moves quickly, and with arms outstretched.

Comments: This game may be played outdoors or indoors. It originated as a game for the swimming pool. It sometimes happens that a slow Marco cannot begin to catch a fast Polo. When this occurs, the teacher may make the circle smaller, or set a time limit.

8. / Form Box

For:

Increasing tactile awareness. (Remember that temporarily eliminating visual clues also strengthens visual perception.)

Practicing elementary skills of categorizing and classifying according to size, shape, texture, pattern, function, distance.

Vocabulary development: using words, such as larger, smaller; square, round; corners, edges; close together, apart; above, below; beside; rough, smooth; etc.

Age: The game is easily varied, from extremely simple versions for young or handicapped children to extremely difficult versions.

Materials:

(1) A medium-sized cardboard box, without a lid, turned on its side, and with two holes cut in the bottom for insertion of hands into the box. The holes should be about four inches apart and just big enough for the hands to go through (so the child will not be tempted to peek through the holes).

(2) Various items for the child to feel, manipulate and identify, depending on which version of the game is being played.

Directions:

Version 1. (Identifying Common Objects.) The simplest version for the young child, or for warm-up for the older child, is identifying common household or classroom objects one at a time, such as: spoon, pencil, blunt scissors, a cup, a toothbrush, a comb, etc. To make the game still easier, show all objects to the children first. A variation to begin discrimination work according to function: place two or more objects in the box for the child to feel, for example, a pencil and a toothbrush. Tell the child to "show me the one you write with." Further, the teacher might ask, "What do we call that object?" (pencil); "Show me how you use it." (Child pantomimes with or without the pencil.)

Version 2. (Identifying Shapes.) Using only those shapes with which the child is somewhat familiar, place a large template (stencil) into the box for the child to feel and identify. To make the game easier, show the child all the shapes which might be used, first. Also you may allow the child to look at a picture of all the basic shapes and identify the one he felt by pointing. As the child becomes more proficient, he can do without the picture, and, still more difficult, he may draw the shape he felt on the chalkboard. To make this version even more challenging, use a smaller template, a block, or a bead; use two similar objects and have child say which is larger; use two textures and say which is rougher; or identify a number or letter that has been cut out of cardboard. Another rather difficult variation is to feel a bead pattern in the box, for example a round bead, a square bead, a cylindrical bead. Withdraw the hands and reproduce the same pattern with other beads.

Version 3. (Block Patterns) (Illustrated.) Glue parquetry or any type of blocks of varying shapes onto a card. (Provide a blank card and loose identical blocks on top of the box.) The blocks may be glued onto the card in any pattern, from very easy (a single square block), to medium-hard (a square and a triangle, one above the other), to difficult (three or more blocks in a vertical or horizontal row). The child feels the glued block pattern on the card (in the form box), removes her hands from the box and makes a duplicate pattern on the blank card on top of the box with the loose blocks.

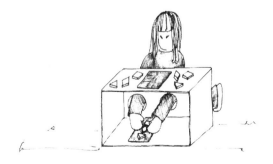

Form Box

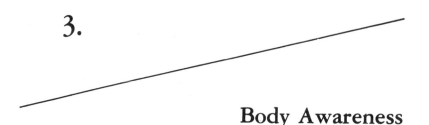

3.

Body Awareness

Physiologists tell us that the underpinnings of much basic learning are closely related to the child's sense of self as a physical being. For example, when the child stands up straight, he or she learns the idea of up and down or vertical (though not necessarily the words). When she lies down, she learns horizontal, or side to side. She comes to realize that all the objects in the world have dimensions and shapes, just as she has. The world of space around the self is seen as a projection of the self. In addition, becoming aware of eyes, ears, nose, and mouth, helps the child realize she can turn her senses on and learn more from them.

9. / Pretzels

The game develops:

> Body awareness: experimenting with tangled-up positions.
> Control of the body: holding the body immobile.
> Differentiation and contraction of specific body parts.

Age: All. Older children will have a greater ability to differentiate body parts.

Materials: None

Directions: "Pretend you are going to make pretzels. Pretend you have a giant mixing bowl there on the floor in front of you. First we pick up a make-believe bag of flour and dump a lot of it into the bowl. Next we add yeast, eggs, milk, some butter and a little salt. Then we stir it all hard until your arms are tired."

"Now *you're* going to be the pretzel. We're going to roll out the dough into long strips and wrap them up in new ways to make some new-fangled pretzels. Wrap-up your arms and legs and head and body any way at all and hold yourself tightly in that fixed position, while you bake. I'm going to go around the room and pull on an arm here, a leg there, and maybe even a head or a foot. I might try to pick up a whole pretzel and move it. If the pretzel can be unwound or bent, it isn't done yet, and must bake a little longer. If it *doesn't* move when I push or pull, it's done, and I'll slide the whole pretzel over to the side of the room, which is the display case. There someone may come in and buy you," etc., etc.

Variation: "Pretend you're a frozen leaf."

Comments: Children love this game, and love the attention of being touched, pushed, pulled or lifted by the teacher. I am always a bit surprised that many bright children have no idea how to contract specific muscles. (The teacher needs to lower expectations for these children and give some extra help.) The game is an excellent one for body awareness and for putting the brain in charge of the body. Both these skills are important for hyperactive, as well as for normally active children.

Obviously, the more simple the position, the easier it will be for the child to differentiate and control a single body part.

Pretzels

10. / Body Touch

For:

Body awareness: body parts, areas, distances and spaces, in and on the body.
Language development: body parts, vocabulary of position (on, around, higher, lower, here, there).

Age: All ages.

Materials: None for the main version. For some versions: a bean bag, a ball, a rope, or other small objects.

Directions: The major body parts should be touched with both hands on command. (With very young children it is more fun to use a simplified Simon Says command. In the simplified version, Simon says practically *every* command.) Older children could play a real Simon Says game (with some minor penalty).

The following body parts should be included in the list: head, hair, eyes, ears, nose, mouth, cheeks, chin, neck, chest, back, stomach, arms, legs, thumb, fingers, knees, feet, toes, hands.

After these are learned, add: ankles, hips, eyebrows, shoulders, sides.

Then: tongue, teeth, waist, thighs, calves, wrists, eyelashes, palms, soles, etc.

Variations:
1. Each child may take a turn giving a command.
2. Bean bag pass-around: have child slide the bean bag *around* his neck, without lifting it off his skin; all *around* the waist, knee, ankle, etc.
3. Rope Knot Touch: fold a jump rope in half, tie a large knot, use the knot as above for body parts touch.

Body Touch

4. Ball Touch: touch body parts with large or small ball. Roll the ball up or down the body.

5. Bean Bag Balance: "Rest the bean bag on your shoulder, and don't move while I count to 10."

6. Touch body parts with feather, piece of fur, stick, pebble, pencil, eraser, even a blade of grass. Any new object will add a new dimension.

Comments: In order to grow, every child needs a deep, continuing sense of self. We are trying to develop a sense of: the permanence, the predictability, and (paradoxically) the variability of the body's many helping parts.

11. / Match My Position

For:

Body awareness (arranging body parts precisely).
Left and right awareness.
Ability to inhibit.
Ability to match a visual stimulus (a model) with one's own body.
Vocabulary (directional words; body parts; same-different).

Age: The matching of position may be more gross (or approximate) for young children; quite precise (even to facial expression or finger placement) for older or adept children.

Materials: For the first version of game, none. For the second version, a cardboard figure or Halloween skeleton, put together with brads so that arms, legs and head are moveable. (A doll would do.)

Directions:
Version 1. The teacher starts out as the leader; later children can take turns leading. The leader starts out by saying "Do what I do," and then, with children watching, slowly arranges his or her body in any simple position, for example: sit with legs crossed Indian style, and with hands clasped behind head. Children copy. The leader then shifts the body to a new position saying, "Match my new position." When children have got the idea, the leader may say, "Now close your eyes tightly while I count to five. Then open your eyes and see if you can figure out what small change I have made in my position. The change may be a large one—I may change an arm or leg—or the change may be very small—I may only lift one finger, or change my facial expression. When you have figured out what the change is, do it, but don't tell anyone. We'll see how many of you can figure out the secret."

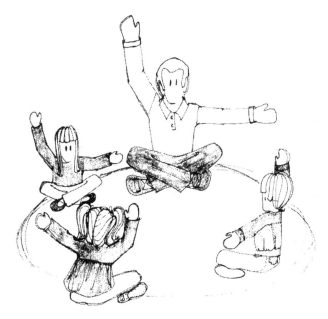

Match My Position

Version 2. Show the children a large or small cardboard figure put together with brads, or better still, have children make their own. Discuss the body parts and how they move. The figure can do some things that we can't, and we can do many things the figure can't. Finally, arrange the figure in various positions and have the class get into the identical position. The game becomes more difficult if arms or legs are crossed.

Comments: These two versions of the Match My Position game provide abundant opportunity for verbal discussion (and vocabulary extension) of body parts and directions. The child will be hearing, for example, "One arm goes straight up toward the ceiling and the other arm points toward the door"; he will be *feeling* these words as he hears them, and will be *seeing* the words acted out by the leader and his classmates.

Remember that the average child is not able to name left and right on himself until about age six. This does not mean that we should postpone teaching left and right at earlier ages; it does mean that we must slowly build right and left awareness while keeping expectations low.

Depending on the ability of the children, the teacher probably should expect *mirroring* of left or right. Older children who know left and right might be asked to *reverse* the leader's right and left, i.e., if the teacher points south with the right hand, children will point north with their right hands.

See also Mirrors, p. 85; Magazine Statues, p. 97.

12. / Busy Bee

For:

Awareness of the body in various new positions.
Following a simple sequence of directions.
Quick response to signal.
Problem solving involving the body and space.

Age: All ages. Very easy as well as difficult versions are given.

Materials: A seven- or eight-foot length of rope for each child will make the game easier and more orderly.

Now touch right ear,
an elbow and a toe to
the rope. No bee could
ever do that!

Busy Bee

Directions:

Version 1 (easiest). Each child takes a length of rope and makes his own "house" with it (a circle on the floor), allowing a little room around it. The teacher then gives directions, "Touch your hand to the rope (or chalk line, or rug). Take hand off the rope and touch your knee to the rope. Remove your knee and touch elbow to the rope. Now try touching your ear to the rope. When you hear the signal 'Busy Bee' quickly change houses (circles) with anyone." Repeat with new directions, calling "Busy Bee!" from time to time.

Version 2. Same as above, but child *keeps* hand on rope, and adds knee. Keeping both hand and knee on rope, child touches elbow to rope. Holding hand, knee and elbow on rope, child maneuvers into a position so as to touch the ear to rope, too. After three or four parts are touching the rope, call "Busy Bee!"

Version 3. Partners: Each *pair* of children arranges their rope "houses" so that the ropes are touching. This makes an "apartment house." Each child sits in his or her side of the apartment house. Now children touch each other as the teacher calls, "hand to hand." After a moment, children drop hands. The teacher calls, "toe to toe." Children touch toes, hold a moment, and get ready for the next command: "thumb to thumb," or "ear to ear," etc. Now and then the teacher calls, "Busy Bee" and all children leave their rope apartment houses and find a new one with a new partner.

Variation: To add an element of suspense and slight competition for older children, designate a chair or one rope circle, off to the side, as the doghouse. There should be one fewer rope houses than children. When children change houses on the signal "Busy Bee," one child will be left over. This child must take one short turn in the doghouse, until the next "Busy Bee!" signal.

Comments: The game may be easily stopped if children are tiring. Preferably stop before they run out of enthusiasm.

By adding "left or right" to any of the commands, all versions of the game become more difficult. Young children should mark their right hands with a rubber band.

For increased body awareness and language enrichment, the teacher might comment frequently on the various positions and methods that children devise in order to solve the problems encountered in the game.

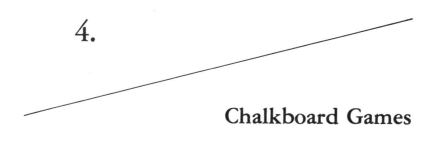

4.

Chalkboard Games

A chalkboard is certainly one of the most versatile and instructive toys a child can have. Few of the everyday motions that children make provide instant feedback as to what exactly that motion was. A chalk and chalkboard leave "tracks," so if the child is trying to make a circle, he can tell if he was successful, and if he made a slip, where exactly that slip occurred. From the first scribble to lines, pictures, designs, printing or writing, no move at the chalkboard is ever wasted. Certain chalkboard activities are especially useful in learning eye-hand coordination, and pre-writing or writing skills.

13. / Stencils

The game develops:

> Shape recognition.
> Eye-hand coordination.
> Arm-hand-finger strength (the handwriting muscles).
> Small space and distance discrimination and judgment.

Age: All ages.

Materials: Chalkboard and chalk; large stencils in the five basic shapes: circle, square, triangle, rectangle, diamond. These can be made of heavy cardboard, formica, masonite, or purchased from school or toy catalogues.

Stencils

Directions: "Holding the circle stencil firmly, and bracing it on the edge of the chalkboard, draw clockwise around the inside of the stencil five times continuously, pushing firmly against the edge. Remove the stencil and try to draw a circle as much like the stencil as possible. Measure the new one with the stencil to see how close you can come."

Repeat counterclockwise. Repeat both directions using the nonpreferred hand. (Yes, we want some skill and versatility in *both* hands. No, it won't cause a dominance problem.)

Variations:
1. Decorate the drawings. Make a face, house, car.
2. Use several stencils; make a picture or design.
3. Find basic shapes in the room (door, window, clock, etc.).
4. Draw a shape with dot-to-dot guides instead of stencil.
5. Make a puzzle by drawing shapes on top of shapes. (See Chalkboard Treasure Hunt, Chapter 25.)
6. Use the stencils (or smaller ones) with paper and pencil.
7. Identify stencils by feel, with eyes closed.

Comments: Really seeing, knowing, and making the basic shapes, and becoming aware of small variations in them, is a fundamental part of reading readiness.

All the numbers and letters, as well as most objects, are composed visually of parts of the basic shapes.

14. / Simon's Race Track

For:

> Strengthening handwriting muscles, and coordinating their movements with the eyes. Making these movements flexible and fluid.
> Quick reactions.
> Left and right awareness.
> Thinking, seeing, hearing, doing, simultaneously.

Age: All ages. Simplify rules for young children.

Materials: Chalk and chalkboard.

Directions: Make a racetrack for each child (a circle about two feet in diameter). There's a "fence" around the outside and a circle of "grass" in the center. The "car" (chalk) must not cross any of the fences. Sample commands:

"Now get your cars on the starting line (top of circle). Don't do anything until Simon tells you. If *I* tell you, don't do it." (Optional: if child forgets three times, he must drop out of game for one turn.)

"Simon says start moving your car to the right (or toward the window).

Simon says reverse directions (or to the left, or toward the door).

Simon says stop.

Simon's Race Track

Simon says go fast, or slow.
Simon says make a heavy line, a light line.
Simon says make a zig-zag line, a dotted line, etc."

Comments: Children under six should not be expected to know right and left correctly, but it's good to practice the *idea* of two sides, and gradually to start naming these sides left and right. If you're buying a chalkboard for the home, don't bury it in the basement or fix it in the child's room. Better a largish portable one that the child can carry around the house, and use standing, sitting or even lying on the floor.

15. / Dog And Squirrel

For:

Visual steering of the hand toward a precise target (aim).
Rapid processing of visual information: space-distance judgments.
Perceptual awareness (figure-ground and form constancy discrimination).
Integration of kinesthetic and visual information.

Age: The game has appeal for all ages and is adjusted instantly to any level. Older children play a fast game where lines cross over one another a great deal. A simplified version employs small circles instead of dots, only a little overlap of lines, and more time to think and plan.

Dog And Squirrel

Materials: Chalkboard and chalk.

Directions: This is a moving dot-to-dot game for two people. Ideally one player should be an adult, to provide verbal feedback. One person is the dog and the other, the squirrel. The dog gets the greater workout.

Pretend that the squirrel comes over to the dog and teases her into a chase. Each jump by the squirrel is marked by a dot. (For young children, draw a small circle instead of a dot.) The dog's path is marked by a straight chalk line. Each time the squirrel makes a dot, the dog draws a straight line to that dot. As soon as the dog connects her line to a dot, the squirrel quickly jumps somewhere else and makes a new dot. The dog continues her line to the new dot, and so it continues all over the chalkboard, with dots and lines alternating in quick succession. Finally, the squirrel runs up a tree and the chase ends, or roles are reversed.

Whenever a child works at the chalkboard, it is important that she stand back from her work and look at the traces from a slight distance, so that she may observe the "tracks" and see her work as a whole unit. Particularly during this game, the child may only be aware of dots and lines. When she stands back to look at the whole, however, she will see that an interesting pattern has taken shape. If there has been much overlap and criss-cross of lines, many large and small triangles, and perhaps some diamonds will have formed among the chalk tracks. Now it is time to play a new game, "Find the Triangles," using the chalk traces. This activity works directly on figure-ground and form constancy discrimination skills. The child (or children) looks for and outlines, possibly with colored chalk, as many triangles as can be found. Children may take turns outlining triangles, and should be encouraged to hunt for all the small, partially hidden triangles.

Comments: Every child will learn from and enjoy this game. It sharpens aim; that is to say, the eyes (via the brain) steer the hands precisely. The chalk's "tracks" give instant visual feedback as to whether the target (dot) was hit or missed.

16. / Sponges

For:

> Strengthening, coordinating and loosening the arm, hand, wrist and shoulder musculature that is (or will be) used in writing.

Age: All ages can benefit. Older children will be expected to handle the sponges more skillfully and creatively.

Materials: Chalkboard, plastic cup for water, and cut-up squares of synthetic household sponge, about 1-1/2 " × 1-1/2" × 3/4".

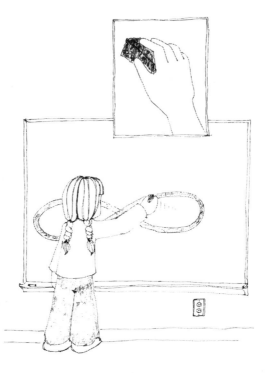

Sponges

Directions: Sponges should be damp-wet, not dripping. Plastic cups should hold only a couple of teaspoons of water to prevent dripping and to encourage the child to focus on his drawn lines rather than on the water. (Another time, with plenty of newspapers handy to catch the drips, the child should have a chance to slosh, drizzle, and drip with the sponges and a lot more water.)

After the child has grown tired of making large circles with chalk (hopefully with each hand separately, and both together), he may make circles with the little wet sponges, adding onto the information and skill he obtained through chalk circles, and adding a new dimension or "feel" to the exercise. He will find that his attempts to obtain rhythmic, and even loose arm movements will be easier with the sponges.

In addition to making large, smooth circles, the child may try a horizontal figure-eight motion, sweeping widely to left and right. The young child may *not* obtain smooth and rhythmic motions with chalk *or* sponges, and should be encouraged to use the sponges in the best way that he can. Instruction should be given, but demands should be kept minimal. All ages of children also should be encouraged to draw designs and pictures with sponges, after doing the rhythmic exercises.

See The Elastic Eight, p. 143.

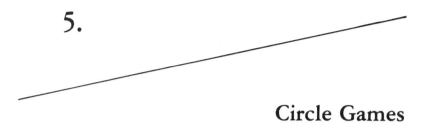

5.

Circle Games

Circle games are so taken for granted that we forget that young children have to learn them. More often than you'd think, many children do not know how to go about them. These may be the children who are labelled unsocial or slow-thinking, when, in fact, they have not absorbed the skills involved in cooperative games.

With very young children, a rope or chalk circle on the floor or ground will keep the circle members from crowding together.

17. / Drop The Flag

The game develops:

Ability to follow simple rules.
Social skills.
Memory: picking a classmate who hasn't had a turn.
Changing pace from slow to fast.
Agility: quick reaction to a visual signal.

Age: All ages.

Materials: A bandana, scarf, or bean bag for the flag. A rope or string about ten to twelve feet long to mark the circle is helpful but not necessary.

Directions: The child who is "It" walks around the outside of the circle of children. She drops the flag behind the feet of a classmate, who picks it up and chases "It" back to the vacant spot in the circle. Even if Child #2 catches Child

Drop The Flag

#1, the turn is passed on; Child #2 becomes the new "It." The new "It" must drop the flag behind a classmate who hasn't had a turn.

Even those children who are not running, learn from watching the runners, predicting where the flag might be dropped, and noting the sequence and rhythm of events of the game.

Comments: Of course, this is the "Drop the Handkerchief" game from time immemorial. It's still fun, easy, and a useful learning device. Young children may need help finding the empty space.

18. / Duck, Duck, Goose

For:

> Social skills: following simple rules; taking turns; picking a friend who hasn't had a turn.
> Changing pace from slow to fast.
> Listening and agility: reacting quickly to a verbal signal.

Age: All ages. Young children may need some help in deciding when to say "Goose."

Materials: None. A twelve-foot rope to mark the circle is helpful.

Directions: Children stand in a circle except for "It." Once the game is learned, and if the class is large, there could be several circles, so that everyone gets a turn.

The child who is "It" walks around the outside of the circle, tapping each child on the shoulder, and saying "Duck." After tapping not more than five or six

Duck, Duck, Goose

ducks, he or she must tap someone, saying "Goose!" and then Goose chases "It" back to the empty spot in the circle.

Whether or not "It" is caught, the turn passes to a new "It," who must pick someone who hasn't had a turn. (Optional for older children: if "It" is caught, she must go into the center of the circle, the "Stewpot," and stay there until someone else is caught.)

Comments: A very popular game with all ages. These children who have had a turn do not lose interest, as in some games. And those who have had a turn still learn by watching the runners, listening for the signal, predicting who will be the next Goose, and watching the sequence and rhythm (organization) of the game. The game is so popular, the teacher should be cautioned not to overuse it.

19. / Rig-A-Jig-Jig

For:

Locomotor patterns: walking, running, galloping, skipping.
Clapping rhythm.
Quick changes: from slow to fast to stop, and repeat. Singing slowly and quietly; change to loud and fast.

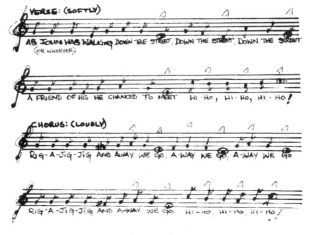

Rig-A-Jig-Jig

Social skills: picking a partner; remembering who has not had a turn; waiting
   to be picked.
Listening for signals.
Extending attention span.

Age: Primarily kindergartners and pre-schoolers.

Materials: None. A rope on the floor to mark the circle is helpful but not
necessary.

Directions: Children stand in a circle except for Child #1, who walks around
the outside of the circle. The group sings the verse very softly and slowly (almost a
whisper, no clapping).
   The word "friend" is a signal for Child #1 to pick a partner (someone who
has not had a turn). The two run, (or gallop, or skip) around the circle. Child #1
heads for Child #2's empty space. As they run, the group begins to clap, singing
the chorus loudly and fast.

Comments: It is important to remind children that they are not racing or
chasing one another, just running together. If the teacher holds a finger to his or
her lips before the start of the verse, it reminds young children it's time to sing
softly. With some young children, the teacher will have to help the runner find the
empty space in the circle.

This old favorite is loaded with learning, and is particularly useful for perseverative children who have trouble changing activities or speeds.

Though there is no competition, children are intrigued by the game and watch each performer attentively as he or she moves around the circle. I have known teachers to get bored with its repetitiveness, but not children.

20. / Rat Trap

For:

Social skills: following simple rules, getting caught, no chiseling, impulse control, and catching classmates in a gentle way.
Auditory skills: quickly reacting to signal.
Spatial information: following a path in and out of "traps."

Age: Ideally suited to the primary age child. Younger children will be able to play quite easily with a little extra help at first.

Materials: A whistle or tom-tom (or any improvised signal device). With young children, a rope or chalk line to mark the circle is very helpful.

Directions: Two or four children are selected to be the trap(s). The pair(s) stands with raised, joined hands, on either side of the circle, so that the circle-path goes under their bridge. All the rats file under the trap and on around the circle. At a whistle or other signal from the teacher, the trap is sprung (trap children lower their arms quickly but gently). Any rat that is caught becomes a part of this trap or a new trap. Continue until all rats are caught.

The teacher should emphasize some simple rules that will make the game very successful:

First, the Trap rules:
1. "When it is your turn to be the trap, you may not lower your arms *except* on the signal.
2. Lower your arms on signal whether or not there are any rats passing beneath.
3. Lower arms quickly but gently, so no one gets bumped."

Next, the Rat rules:
1. "When you are a rat, you may not stop walking, except on the signal.
2. You may not slow down, or run, or duck down, when going under the trap."

The children who started out as traps should be given an opportunity to be

Rat Trap

rats, (after there are some new traps). From time to time, the teacher may close his or her eyes so as not to know who is going under the trap.

Comments: This game is a delight to all children. There is a slight element of suspense, just enough to make it exciting. Because everyone gets caught, there is little pressure to "win." And getting caught does not mean dropping out, only changing to another interesting role.

However, because there are a few simple rules that must be observed to make the game go well, the game presents an ideal opportunity to teach social skills and consideration for one's classmates. If the teacher will review the rules before the game begins—quick but gentle lowering of the trap, no ducking, getting caught gracefully, etc.—and the reasons for these rules, children *will* be considerate and learn at least a little of the pleasures of sportsmanship.

Some young children may become disoriented in going around the circle, and may wander off the path or pass outside the traps. These are usually children with spatial confusions, and they may need some help from the teacher. The rope guide (see Materials) would be helpful for these children.

6.

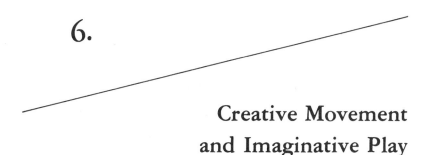

Creative Movement and Imaginative Play

Much of a child's day (whether in school or at home) is spent conforming to the rules of the world. The rules may be people-rules (time to eat, wash your hands, hang up your coat) or nature-rules (when you tip too far to the side, you may fall off your chair; when it's cold you must bundle up; when you stub your toe, it hurts).

Creative movement and/or imaginative, "let's pretend" games give the child a chance to make up his or her own rules, decide at least part of his actions, and delight his friends or himself. Best of all, in this kind of game, there is no right or wrong.

21. / Butterfly In The Cocoon

This game develops:

The ability to act out a simple story sequence (in this case, an elementary science concept).

Body-in-space awareness through overlap of verbal, tactile, visual and kinesthetic cues.

Differentiation, coordination and control of body parts: homolateral and cross-lateral; right and left.

Butterfly In The Cocoon

Age: All ages.

Materials: None.

Directions: (This game is based on angels-in-the-snow movements, wherein a child lies on his back and stretches arms and legs out and back.)

Before you start the game, discuss the word and idea of cocoon and/or chrysalis. Ask if anyone has seen one, or knows what is inside, etc.

1. The egg. "Pretend you're a tiny egg fastened to a leaf that's swaying in the wind. Lie on your back, fold your knees near your chest, and hold them; now rock gently in the breeze."

2. The caterpillar. "When the egg is ready to hatch, out comes a tiny caterpillar. She may be light or dark, fuzzy or smooth, spotted or striped, depending on what type of butterfly she will be. The caterpillar eats, eats, eats, and walks around a little, and grows into a big, fat caterpillar. Get up on your hands and knees, crawl around slowly, and pretend you are nibbling leaves."

3. The pupa (cocoon or chrysalis). "When the caterpillar gets to be nice and fat, she knows it's time to spin her cocoon. (Sit on the floor, lift your feet a little and push yourself in a slow spin.) The caterpillar fastens herself to a twig and spins a long silk thread around and around herself, until she's all wrapped up inside. (Now curl up as small as you can on knees and elbows, head tucked down.) The caterpillar is asleep in her cocoon. The sun shines on her little house, the rain pitter-patters on it too, and inside, something magical is happening. Guess what is happening to the pupa. Wings are growing, with beautiful colors, etc."

4. The butterfly. "When the pupa has finished changing into a butterfly, she knows it is time to break open the cocoon and crawl out. (Pretend to slowly climb out.) She crawls to the twig beside her empty cocoon, and rests there. She is not beautiful yet. Her wings are wrinkled and wet; her legs are weak and wobbly. She spends a whole day exercising her wings and legs, and pumping fluid through them, before she can fly. Lie down on your back, and slowly stretch one wing out and up, sliding your hand along the rug all the way. Now slide your wing back down to your side. Next stretch out one leg, letting your heel slide along the rug (or floor) all the way. Slowly increase speed, and try various patterns (right arm, right leg; left arm, left leg, etc.). Finally move both arms and legs rhythmically, get up and fly away."

Comments: This game, while it has a rather tight structure, is intriguing to children because (1) it is easy to do; and (2) they are almost spellbound by the magic transformation of egg to butterfly. Teachers are fond of it because it has multiple physical benefits. Mainly, it works on a different kind of neurological control wherein the usual effect of gravity is minimized, and a different kind of body feedback is provided.

22. / Things Come To Life

For:

Increasing creativity and the ability to improvise.
Confidence in own ideas, no matter how ordinary they may be.
Body awareness in various positions.
Vocabulary development.
Having fun as a group.

Age: All ages.

A tree in a windstorm

Things Come To Life

Materials: None needed, although pictures or props, poems, stories or records may be used to stimulate ideas.

Directions: Until the teacher gets the feel for group creative play, it is helpful to limit the children's area of movement by giving each a hoop (or rope) "house" to stand in.

The teacher may start the ball rolling by saying, "Let's pretend we're balloons being blown up—start small (stooping) and get bigger and bigger. Stretch to your very biggest. Now let all the air out slowly," etc. As the children get the idea, the teacher may give less and less indication of just *how* to act out an object. Perhaps each child will think up a different way.

Things we could be (using the whole body):

an egg-beater	fire or flames
a rubber ball	popcorn
a cradle	an airplane
a pencil writing on a piece of paper	a slow-motion movie
a tree in a windstorm	a wheel
a rag doll losing its sawdust	a wheelbarrow
a feather or leaf falling	a bulldozer
an ice cube	a needle going through cloth
a feather duster	an electric toothbrush

Variations:

1. One child may demonstrate, others copy.
2. Give the child a picture to act out or let her select her own card from a stack of act-outable objects.
3. Try some unconventional objects: "What can you think of that's red? A tomato? How could you pretend to be one?" etc. "A pan of bubbling tomato sauce? Good, see if you can show us how it would look to be a bubbling sauce pan," etc.

Comments: Some teachers are good at stimulating this kind of self-directed play in a classroom. For others, a group may get out of hand. Creative or dramatic play is an important skill for children to have, and should not be left to free-play time only. There are many hints for insuring successful creative play, such as: allowing children to copy each other if they need to at first; spoon-feeding ideas to a child who can't seem to think up his own; agreeing on a signal which means "freeze where you are"; and of course, the teacher should remain non-judgmental of the quality of all the children's dramatizations. As usual, everyone who participates is a winner.

23. / Simple Charades

For:

Communicating by gesture (body language).
Matching motor actions to visual and verbal stimuli.
Body awareness, social skills, confidence.
Simple imaginative problem-solving ("How can you act out corn-on-the-cob?").
Memory.

Age: Easily varied from simple to complex. As children become more adept, they may move from acting out a single simple object or action to a series of objects, or to increasingly abstract words and ideas.

Materials: A set of 5 × 7 cards (from 10-20), each with a sketch of an object or a simple action that may be communicated through gestures. (Older children might not need the stimulus of pictures.) The following items are suggestions:

1. Kitchen objects: egg-beater, knife and fork, mixing bowl and spoon, cup, pancake turner.
2. Desk or school objects: pencil, scissors, chalk and chalkboard, book.
3. Common sports: skating, bouncing ball, basketball, bowling, etc.

Simple Charades

4. Other common activities and/or objects: brushing teeth (or toothbrush), comb or combing hair, putting on a shoe, sleeping, etc.

Directions: The teacher should explain and demonstrate how we must exaggerate a bit in order to communicate by gesture. Let the child select a card from the pile, preferably with cards turned face down. Next, make sure the child knows how to act it out. The teacher should provide active coaching while children are learning the game. The child acts out the picture before a small or large group of other children who guess what the picture is. The object of the game is for the actor to enable the class to guess in the *shortest* possible time.

Comments: Many otherwise bright children are very poor at figuring out how to interpret or act out objects or facial expressions, or to perform other silent pantomime. For that matter, many children do not know how to go about verbal dramatic play either. Therefore any efforts that the teacher may make along these lines will pay off richly in stimulating and facilitating creative thinking and original use of the imagination, so important later, in many types of problem-solving activities. The teacher may not *see* the results of his or her efforts immediately, but the benefits are there nonetheless.

Variations:
1. For short-term memory: let the child pick two or even three cards; look at them and decide how he will act out the objects, etc.; put the cards away; and then act out the series, in the order in which he selected the cards.

2. For older children: after children become skillful in acting out objects or simple actions, they may begin to act out, for the rest of the classroom to guess, a simple *situation*. This is much more difficult for the child, and will require a series of actions all connected by a single idea. Examples of situations that could be silently pantomimed: (a) making scrambled eggs (getting a skillet, turning on the stove, breaking the eggs, stirring the eggs, spooning them onto a plate and eating); (b) going to a movie (buying a ticket, finding a seat, watching with changing expressions, perhaps eating popcorn); (c) getting up and dressed in the morning (yawning, washing the face, dressing, etc.); (d) some situations involving two or even a small group of children, as going to the circus: two children could be the audience, buying tickets, etc. and two other children could be tightrope walkers, etc.

Older children may be able to think up their own situations, especially in a group.

24. / Teacher-Facilitated Dramatic Play

For:

Exercising social skills and social judgment; communication skills, both verbal and motoric.

Organizing ideas and information, whether fanciful or serious, into a simple or complex sequence.

Language practice.

Confidence in one's ability to improvise, try on new roles, and convey ideas.

Age: Hopefully one never outgrows the ability to role-play and dramatize ideas.

Materials: The ordinary objects in a classroom are generally all that is necessary. However, special props and objects are often stimulating, depending on the type of dramatic activity being enacted.

Introductory comments: Contrary to popular opinion, the ability to role-play and engage in creative dramatic play does not appear automatically. It is a learned behavior in which all too many children are quite unskilled. Children without these skills may be socially isolated or have poor everyday judgment. In some instances, children may *appear* to be mentally obtuse when, in fact, they have not learned to think or express themselves spontaneously. Children from deprived homes, and I include all socio-economic levels, *may* lack the skills of imaginative play and/or creative playfulness. Learning disabled children particularly, even though repeatedly exposed to opportunities for creative play, may fail to absorb the

Teacher-Facilitated Dramatic Play

ability. With patience, such children can be brought along. The payoff is enormous, and not just in social adaptability. Imagination is absolutely necessary in order to associate meaning with printed words and ideas; and even in such a precise subject as mathematics, imagination and creativity are necessary in order to hypothesize and problem-solve. Dramatic play is also a natural wellspring of language development.

Directions: The idea is for the teacher to provide the structure for the situation: think up the idea, assemble props, assign roles and actively model one of the roles. With older children, the teacher may be the movie director and actively coach from the sidelines. The group should be small, particularly with young children, to insure full participation. Gradually the teacher fades out of his or her active role and becomes the audience as the children take over. This fading process may take five minutes or five months, or longer, depending on the ages and abilities of the children. The progress and structure of the play may rest almost entirely on the teacher, even to the extent that he or she tells the child what to say and do; and/or the teacher may provide only occasional intervention. The goal, of course, is to teach the children how to get in touch with and express their natural flow of mental images. This is no small accomplishment.

Some examples:

1. Perhaps start with playing house, store, or job roles, such as fireman, policeman, teacher, beautician. Hopefully it will be emphasized that adult jobs are less and less sex-typed, and increasingly available to both sexes.

2. Enact a nursery rhyme, a simple story, or part of a movie. (See Simple Charades, p. 53.)

3. Re-enact a trip the class took, for example, let some children take turns being the tour guide on "a trip through a bakery."

4. Role-play an open-ended, controversial or difficult situation that has occurred or might occur: going to the dentist or hospital; a child scolded in the dime store for handling the merchandise; a classmate cheating or hurt in a playground game; expression of feelings of humor, affection, etc.

5. Re-enact, explaining as you go along, a task where a more or less precise sequence of steps is important, for example, packing for a picnic; starting a car and going on a trip; preparing for a party; preparing a meal; having a car or an airplane race.

6. Whimsical or free-rein imaginative play, for example, "Pretend you're on a magic carpet. You can go anywhere; what will you see down on the ground?" "Pretend you have a magic wand; you can do anything." "Pretend you can have any wish; what would you choose?" etc.

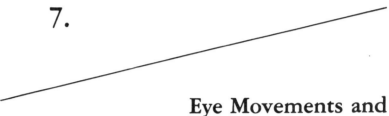

7.

Eye Movements and Eye-Hand Coordination

In our zeal for physical fitness, we often forget that the eyes are moved too, each by six tiny muscles. These muscles may be poorly coordinated just as biceps may, through lack of proper use.

Many children enter school with adequate visual acuity but with poor visual ability to: 1) track a slowly moving object, 2) guide the hand, foot, or body, or 3) focus quickly on a near or far object. Very often these children, whose eyes are not serving them well, cannot pay steady, relaxed attention to any visual stimulus, including the teacher.

25. / Balloon Volley Ball

The game develops:

Visual tracking skills, near and far focus; eye-hand, eye-foot, eye-body coordination. (See variations below.)

Space-judging (also time, speed, distance, force concepts).

Balance and agility (in a looking-up position).

Body awareness (see variations); right and left awareness.

Response to auditory signals.

Object handling skills.

Balloon Volley Ball

Age: All ages.

Materials: One large *round* balloon for each pair of children. A tom-tom. Rope(s) or string line(s) on the floor are helpful to divide the area into courts. A yardstick also makes an adequate center line.

Directions: Keep rules simple. It is generally more fun to omit keeping score. Hit the ball as many times as needed to get it across the line. Young children may have to be taught how to "spank" the balloon, instead of catching and throwing it. If the balloon goes into a neighbor's court, go behind the neighbor to retrieve it.

Variations: When the tom-tom sounds, balloon play freezes. "Now, hit the balloon with the left hand only; then right only, then alternate. Next, kick the balloon across the line; right foot only, etc. Later, hit the balloon with thumb, fist, wrist, ankle, elbow, forehead, forefinger, the left side of your body," etc.

Comments: Surely one of the most versatile, useful and most fun games of all.

And it works on the important eye skills that are hard to develop. (Most young children cannot begin to handle a fast-moving airborn ball.)

Many children start the game with a blank look. Within five seconds they are smiling and laughing.

26. / Spinning Ball

For:

Increasing control of eye muscles by tracking a moving object.
Identifying common objects from partial visual clues.
Following simple rules of the game.

Age: Primary age children.

Materials: A wiffle ball tied to the end of a short length of rope. A ten-inch piece of masking tape around the circumference of the ball. (Preferably use gym floor marking tape, available at sporting goods stores, as it holds its "stick" longer.)

A few bright colored, light weight, familiar objects or toys to tape to the ball, such as chalk, pencil, a block, a wad of yarn, a small puppet, a spoon, a deflated balloon, etc. (Objects should be about three inches to six inches long, one or two inches wide.)

Directions: The point of the game is *not* really to identify the objects, but to give the children eye exercise and to maintain their interest while they are tracking. To introduce the game, have the children sit on the floor with their backs to a wall. Show all the objects to the children first, then keep the objects hidden in a box. Spin the ball as slowly as possible the first time, with a very easy-to-identify object fastened onto it, to give the children an idea of how it feels to track a ball in a circular path.

"Now that we've had a practice run, we're ready to really play the game." Tell the children they are to turn to the wall and close their eyes while you fasten an object (for example, a spoon) to the ball and get it spinning. When you say, "Everyone look now!" children turn around and watch the spinning ball and try to mentally identify the object. When each child thinks he knows what the object is, he again turns around and faces the wall.

For those children who have great difficulty tracking, I slow the ball down, almost to a stop, so they will be encouraged to keep trying. This is after the other children have turned to the wall.

When all children are facing the wall, stop the ball and say, "Turn around again, and let's talk about the object. Jane, was it a pencil? Mark, was it a pen?

Spinning Ball

Karen, was it a balloon? Jim, was it a spoon?" You will soon have a good idea who really can identify and who has trouble consistently. Those who move their heads or cannot identify should have extra practice with all sorts of bean-bag, ball, and moving object games.

Comments: Children get the hang of tracking the spinning ball quite quickly. The first few games may be difficult, so give plenty of hints.

It is reassuring to know that eye muscles may respond to exercise, just as other muscles. You cannot hurt the eyes by having a child track. However, the game requires intense concentration and I would suggest that it be limited to five or six minutes. Watch for children who must move their heads instead of their eyes. These children need extra visual practice.

27. / Peripheral Vision Game

For:

Awareness of the visual field at the sides of the body.
More efficient use of eye musculature and acuity.
Identification of objects through minimal visual cues.

Attention and concentration.

Some body and spatial awareness.

Age: All ages are readily intrigued by this game. Younger children should play a slower, shorter game, and the objects they are asked to identify should be familiar ones, of larger size and/or brighter color.

Materials: A chair and a box of objects, preferably brightly colored, such as a pencil, a marker, a ball, a card, a ruler, a block, a small ball of yarn, a large feather, a bandana, any small toys.

Directions: The child sits on a chair facing the class. The teacher stands behind the child, with one hand resting lightly on the child's head, to remind him *not* to turn his head; the child may turn his *eyes* as far to the left or right as he wishes. Holding a brightly-colored object in her hand, the teacher says, "I'm going to bring this object up from behind your head, at eye level, on the right side (or left). It will slowly move into your field of side vision. When you can see the color of the object, tell us what color. I will continue to move the object forward. When you think you can identify the object, tell us, and I will tell you if you're right. If you're right, we'll place it on the floor directly beneath the place where you identified it."

The child should compete only with himself. Anyone who identifies the object within a reasonable distance is praised. Older children may be permitted to

Peripheral Vision Game

compete a bit; but in this case, children may be reminded, briefly but specifically, how to be appreciative of *all* their classmates' efforts.

Variations: Children who know their basic shapes might identify drawings of these from cards. Children might identify letters, numbers, words (written on cards), but care should be taken that there is a ninety-percent success rate for each child.

A quite difficult version, for older children with good concentration, is to have the child identify objects while keeping the *eyes* focused straight ahead (i.e., neither eyes nor head may be turned).

Comments: This is a good game for children who turn their heads instead of their eyes when reading or following any moving object.

This activity could come under the category of eye exercise. Some perceptual-motor psychologists cast doubt on the value of such exercises. It is my opinion that they *are* valuable. At the very least this game will increase the child's attention span.

28. / Bubbles

For:

> Certain delicate hand movements, peculiar to the task, are required for making and releasing bubbles.
> There is endless purposeful guiding of the hands with the eyes, ocular tracking, and near and far focusing of the eyes. (Children repeatedly focus two feet away for dipping, close to the face for blowing, two feet away for freeing the bubble. Then, if the bubble does not burst, children may continue to track the bubble, sometimes for considerable distances.)
> Social skills: courtesies and consideration.

Age: All ages.

Materials: A variety of juice cans, soup cans, etc. with *both* ends cut out; at least one can for each child. Bubble solution made of 50% liquid dishwashing detergent and 50% water. Enough plastic bowl-shaped dipping containers so that each group of two or three children may have one. Hopefully, the bowls will be fairly resistant to tipping.

Directions: The teacher should demonstrate how to dip one end of the can into the detergent solution, to make sure that a "window" is formed on the end; how to blow through the tube; how to twist the can gently to dislodge the bubble into the

Bubbles

air. It is important that a few courtesy rules be discussed *before* going outside, for example, "No child may break another child's bubble, but you may chase and break your own if you want. Bowls should be placed where they will not be stepped on or tipped over. Children should be careful not to blow bubbles near other children's faces. Children may have to wait briefly for a turn to dip."

Variations: Children should experiment with various sizes of cans, and with gentle or fast methods of blowing the bubbles. Small bubbles may be blown with plastic drinking straws; multiple bubbles, by dipping six-ringed plastic six-pack carriers into a tray of bubble solution.

Comments: Expect high enthusiasm and considerable healthy noise. If the teacher wants to work on social skills, this activity lends itself readily to such a discussion. In the discussion, which should be brief, indoors and prior to the activity, the teacher might ask, "What should you do if you want to dip the can in the bubble solution and someone is already dipping? Should you push that person aside?" (Children will decide that one should wait quietly a moment or two for a turn.) Teacher: "What should you do if someone else's great big bubble floats right past your hand and you're dying to reach out and pop it?" (The answer, of course, is to let it go on by, and pop your *own* bubbles if you want.)

During and after bubble play, the teacher should notice and reinforce considerate behavior.

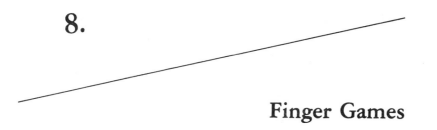

8.

Finger Games

Much more than a diversion, finger games require refined movements of the small muscles of the fingers, hands, and sometimes arms or legs. The marshalling and exercising of the brain control system is the same as that needed in large muscle control.

Finger games have the advantages of fitting into small snatches of time, uniting a group in a common entertainment; and they are certainly easy to take along in the car. Often they are the vehicles for basic intellectual concepts.

29. / Slap-Clap-Snap

The game develops:

Coordination and control of small hand and finger muscles.
Simultaneous match of rhythm-words-actions-visual monitoring.
Vocabulary and categories.
Socializing: unifying a group.
Body awareness.

Age: Primary ages and kindergartners. Three's and four's may do a slow-motion version.

Materials: None.

Directions: Sit in circle. Practice very slowly the sequence:
1. Slap thighs.

Slap-Clap-Snap

2. Clap hands.
3. Snap fingers (or rub thumb and middle finger together).
4. Rest briefly, then repeat all steps.

When all participants get the rhythm going, stop a moment and explain that we are going to go around the circle and say *together* each child's first name, *at the exact moment of the snap*.

When this has been mastered, we'll go around and each child will say his or her name *alone, on the snap*.

The next stage: We'll go around and say together our numbers, on the snap (or older children, multiples of five).

Next each child may think of a color. Make sure each child has a color in mind before starting the rhythm. On *snap*, each child takes a turn saying a color.

You might have each child take a turn naming a food; individuals may name fruits, vegetables, desserts (a favorite category), cars, flavors, words that begin with "b," multiples of seven, sports, in fact any category. (Only one category should be used in the game at a time.)

Comments: It is not necessary that children produce an actual snap of the fingers—just rub thumb and finger together.

30. / The Brave Indian Brave (Or Girl)

For:

Translating words into gestures; establishing a rhythm or continuous flow of gestures; listening for signals; quick changes; changing pace from slow to fast.

Combining words with specific gestures.

Age: All ages.

Materials: None. The teacher will be reassured by having the script in front of her the first few times. Eventually she can improvise, changing phrases around, adding phrases, etc.

Directions: Explain what an Indian brave is. Explain each gesture: "Every time you hear the word Indian, put a feather in your hair, like this. (One finger sticks up beside head.) You try it."

Actions:

    Bear: lift outstretched hands up, purse lips.
    Walking: slap thighs with hands, alternately.
    See: shade eyes with hand.
    Bridge: pound chest with fist.
    Jump: raise hands above head.
    Swim: brush palms together.
    Slams the gate: clap.
    Runs: slap legs very fast.
    Indian: hold finger to head like feather.

Story: Once upon a time there was a brave *Indian* brave. He said to his *Indian* friends, "I am going hunting to find a grizzly *bear*. So he *walked* out the gate and he *slammed* it. He hadn't *walked* far until he *saw* a rabbit; but he didn't *see* a *bear*—so he *walked* on.

He came to a *bridge* and he *walked* across. He hadn't *walked* far until he *saw* a deer; but he didn't *see* a *bear* . . . so he *walked* on.

Soon he came to a ditch. He couldn't step across so he backed up. He said, "I *jump* ditch!" He started to *run* . . . faster . . . faster . . . faster! He *j-u-m-m-m-m-m-ped* and he landed on the other side. Then he *walked* on. He came to a river. He *jumped* in and *swam* across. Then he *jumped* out and *ran* on. All of a sudden he came face to face with a great big *bear*. W-o-o-o-w!

He turned around and he *ran* down the hill. He *jumped* into the river and *swam* across. He *jumped* out and he *ran* on. He *jumped* over the ditch, and he *ran* on. He *saw* a rabbit, but he *ran* on. He *ran* across the *bridge*. He *saw* a deer, but he *ran* on. When he got home, he *slammed* the gate. And he said, "I *s-s-saw* a *b-b-b-bear*!"

All the other *Indians* said . . . "Ugh!" and that's the story of the brave *Indian* brave.

Variations:

1. Do the whole thing with a brave Indian girl as the central character. It is important that teachers include stories about girls, wherein the girls are involved in a wide variety of adventures and activities. And add stories about intuitive, helpful and tender boys.

all of a sudden,
he came face to face
with a great big bear!

The Brave Indian Brave (Or Girl)

2. The teacher and children could make up a story involving small or large body motions, such as:
   a. "Getting Ready for School" (washing, brushing teeth, dressing, eating breakfast, etc.).
   b. "Going on a Picnic" (washing the apples, counting the spoons, slicing the cheese, spreading the tablecloth, throwing a (make-believe) ball, etc.).
   c. "Going to the Zoo" (do animal walks).
   d. A variation of this game which some teachers may know as "Going on a Lion Hunt."

See Simple Charades, p. 53; Teacher Facilitated Dramatic Play, p. 55.

Comments: The motions are so easy in this long-time favorite game, and the story so intriguing, that the most recalcitrant child will participate happily.

31. / Five Little Monkeys

For:

Following a sequence verbally and motorically.

Matching number words to the corresponding number of fingers.

Age: For pre-schoolers and kindergartners; some first graders.

Materials: None.

Directions:

> Five little monkeys (hold up hand with fingers outstretched)
> Jumping on the bed (bounce fingertips of one hand into palm of other hand)
> One fell off (hold up one finger)
> and bumped his head (place hands on head)
> Called up the doctor (one hand holds telephone to ear, other hand dials)
> and the doctor said,
> "No more monkeys (shake forefinger)
> Jumping on the bed."
>
> Continue with four fingers held up, four fingers bounce, etc. to the "Last Little Monkey."

Variation: With each verse, the doctor's voice becomes softer and softer.

Comments: The story is irresistible, even for the most shy, non-participatory child.

Five Little Monkeys

32. / X Marks The Spot

For:

Eye-hand coordination.
Tactile and kinesthetic awareness of shape and location.
Following precise directions, matching actions and tactile reception to verbal
  signals.

Expressing gentleness and affection.

Age: Older children enjoy this game thoroughly, yet it is not too difficult for three- and four-year-olds.

Materials: None.

Directions: Children play the game in pairs, seated on the floor so that one child may draw on his partner's back. Half the children are "chalks," half are "chalkboards." (Game may later be repeated, with children changing roles.) The teacher should first explain how the various shapes are drawn (perhaps using a real chalkboard for this). It is especially necessary to show young children how to draw a dash and a question mark.

"Chalk" children follow the directions of the poem, exactly as given; "chalkboard" children attempt to visualize the tactile impression they are receiving:

X marks the spot ("chalks" draw a big X on partners' backs)
With a dot and a dot (two gentle horizontal dots)
And a dash and a dash (two horizontal short lines)
And a big question mark (any curved line, with a dot under it).
Tickle up (fingers starting at the lower part of partner's back, up to the nape of the neck and wait there a moment)
Tickle down (fingers down, and wait),
Tickle up (repeat up)
Tickle down (repeat down),
A cool summer breeze (blow gently on partner's hair)
And a soft little squeeze (place hands on partner's shoulders and give a little squeeze or hug).
Children reverse roles. "Chalks" become "chalkboards," and vice versa.

Variations:

1. Substitute other shapes and marks for the X, dots, and other marks: "There's a little circle in the middle, with a great big square around it. On each corner of the square, make a dot. Under the square draw a long line."

2. "Pretend you're throwing a pebble into a pond." (Make a dot gently in the center of partner's back.) "See all the ripples coming from the place where the pebble fell in." (Draw increasing sizes of circles.) "Suddenly a fish jumps out of the water," (draw a line straight up) "and falls back in" (draw a line back down).

3. "Once upon a time some animals were playing on a hill. One at a time they ran down the hill and then walked back up. First there was a wibble-wobble duck who zig-zagged down the hill." (Start at the top of

X Marks The Spot

partner's back and zig-zag down quickly; come back up, zig-zagging slowly.) "Next a kangaroo bounded down in one big jump. A rabbit came with many small bounces. And last, a mouse skittered down with many tiny steps," etc.

4. Try making up your own mini-story, perhaps involving some kind of chase or follow-the-leader action.

Comments: It is important that children press firmly enough that their partners can feel the exact shape of the design being drawn. A more common problem is that some children get carried away and draw more dots, etc. than necessary. For maximum learning, it is important that "chalks" draw exactly what the words specify, i.e., exactly two dots, etc. If the teacher explains ahead that each chalk must do exactly what the words say; and if he or she explains that when the "tickle up" part arrives, the fingers go up and *wait*, children will observe these directions carefully. At the same time, the teacher *must* emphasize the need for gentleness: dots may not be hard pokes, tickles must be light, the "breeze" must be soft, the squeeze needs to be gentle, etc. In other words, with a little time given to directions, the game is very successful on the first try.

9.

Finger, Hand, and Arm Strengtheners

Though fine motor control does not automatically follow gross motor development, there is a strong natural inclination for this to occur. In any event, for either fine or gross control (and coordination) to take place, a certain minimum of muscle strength is required.

It has been observed that many fine motor problems are accompanied by weak, inflexible hand and arm musculature. Therefore our first task is to lay a groundwork of strength, then coordination will almost certainly be easier to establish.

33. / Animal Walks

This game develops:

> Whole body strength, especially of the arms and hands.
> Space and body awareness: comparative "feel" in different positions and spaces.
> Balance, coordination, agility.
> The integration of picture information, actions, and words.

Age: All ages.

Materials: $8'' \times 10''$ cards or papers with stick figures illustrating animal positions. Cards may be crude penciled sketches plus a magazine cutout picture of the animal.

Directions: Select several cards of animal stunts, where a large part of the body's weight is borne by the arms and hands. Examples:

Bear: walk on soles of feet, palms of hands.

Seal or Walrus: lie on stomach, prop the upper body up with stiff arms, pull body along with arms and hands; drag legs.

Crab: sit on the floor, hands behind body. Lift seat and walk on hands and feet.

Snake: advance with stomach flat on floor, and pull self along with hands and forearms, while pushing with legs.

Lame dog: advance on two hands and one foot, or two feet and one hand.

Rabbit (or frog): stoop with hands out in front for support; slide hands forward along the floor, bring feet up toward hands with jumping motion.

Animal Walks

Mule kick: support self on two feet and two hands. From time to time, both feet are kicked up in the air, while supporting body with the hands.

Measuring worm: start in push-up position, with body in a straight line supported by hands and toes. Keeping hands fixed, walk with feet as far as possible. Keeping feet fixed, then "walk" with hands only until body is in a straight line again. Continue alternately walking with hands and feet.

Show the card, talk about the positions while demonstrating them. Let one child also demonstrate and/or let all children practice a moment, then let children walk across or around the room in the style of the animal.

Variations: "Animal Street": using from three to eight pictures of animal stunts listed above, arrange a course around the edge of the room, each card being about ten feet from the next. Children start at any of the various cards, walk like the animal pictured until they get to the next station, and then change position. They may (or may not) pass one another, as the teacher decides.

Comments: Excellent exercise which the most clumsy, un-adept child, as well as the athletic one, can attempt and benefit from. A no-lose game for all seasons, all ages, all degrees of skill.

If I were to go to the South Sea Islands and could take only two pounds of teaching materials, animal cards would make up my first four ounces.

More animal walks can be found in elementary physical education books in the library.

34. / Scooterboards

For:

Bilaterality (using both arms equally).

Body awareness in a different plane.

Whole body strength: especially neck, back, arms and hands.

Posture: good for round-shouldered children. Variation 3 (sitting and being pulled) is good for sway-backed children.

Age: All ages. Young children should do only those variations that are within their instructional level.

Materials: Preferably one scooterboard for each child. Generally, these activities are suitable for small groups of four to eight children.

How to make: half-inch plywood, 11″ × 19″, with casters on each corner (or scooterboards may be purchased through school catalogues).

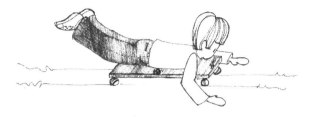

Scooterboards

Directions and variations:

1. Child lies on the scooterboard lengthwise, with the waist at the center of the board. The midsection is supported; the head and legs are held at an angle that is not overly tiring, yet provides excellent exercise for many little-used back muscles. The child rows with the arms; to make the board go straight, he must push with equal force on both sides.

2. Child may lie on back and push with feet or may kneel on hands and knees and push with one foot; in fact, he may ride the board any way except standing. Older children may put hands on board, run a few steps, flop down sled-style and coast.

3. For further hand strength and back strength, child sits on board with knees drawn up, or cross-legged. He bends forward and grasps with both hands *both* the front edge of the scooterboard *and* a rope that can be pulled by another child. If the child maintains a firm grasp, he can be spun in a large, fast circle.

4. Child may lie on stomach on board, with feet braced against a wall; with one big push, see how far he can coast across the room.

5. See how many swimming strokes it takes to get across the room.

6. Have races and relay races.

Comments: Several children on scooterboards have as much fun free-style as if they were at a carnival. Safety rules (no standing, no bumping) should be discussed first. Children are usually careful to observe the safety rules. Those who "forget" are given a summons and must sit in jail for a very few minutes.

35. / Bar Hang And Count

For:

Overall body strength, particularly of the fingers, hands, arms, shoulders.

Bar Hang And Count

Self-confidence.
Time concepts.

Age: All ages. This activity is for building strength and confidence in the many children who are unable to chin themselves or "hand-walk" across a horizontal ladder. Most pre-schoolers and many elementary children fall into this category.

Materials: A doorway chinning (gym) bar, or an overhead ladder. A jungle gym might do in a pinch. A chair to stand on is helpful. A mat (or several layers of carpet) under the bar is important.

Directions and comments: The object of the activity is for the child to hang in straight arm position for increasingly long periods of time. There are many children in our society, who for one reason or another, have extremely poor grip strength; and many of these children also have problems controlling the small muscles of the hands and fingers. These may be the children who have difficulties printing, writing, cutting, pouring, tying, and performing many of the myriad fine-motor tasks that we expect of them, in or out of school. Building hand strength is one way of working on the problem, although this alone will not insure coordination.

    Children with weak hands naturally may avoid or have some fear of hanging on a chinning bar. In addition, many fear dropping from the hanging position to the floor, but if the teacher can manage the time to watch, count, and praise even the most brief hanging attempt, there is generally a dramatic improvement in performing this exercise. For example, it is not unusual for a child to move from hanging only three seconds to thirty seconds in a matter of a few days.

The most non-athletic child very likely will clamor for a turn hanging on the bar, if the teacher watches and counts. There are several fascinating factors at work here that are worth noting: first, the child is receiving the undivided attention of an adult; second, the child is aware that no matter how short the duration of his hang, it will be approved; and third, the child feels supported, both physically and psychologically and knows he can turn that support on or off as needed. (See use of chair below.)

The mystique of "the chair": The smaller the child, the greater is the distance between his feet and the floor; i.e., the more difficult is the drop. It is important, therefore, when a child is first learning to hang from a bar, that he not be asked to learn to drop also. Some means of support should be provided so that as his grip begins to falter, he may regain a standing position quickly. A box under the feet is satisfactory, but this may encourage the child to touch down too soon. Ideally, we want a support that can be withdrawn while the child hangs, and replaced as the child's grip falters. A chair is very useful in this situation. One method which works well is to tell the child, "Start by standing on this chair until you get a good grip on the bar. As you swing free, I will slide the chair out of your way and I will start to count. *Whenever* you need the chair replaced, just call, 'Chair!' and I'll slide it under your feet immediately." Children are delighted with this arrangement, feel very much supported, and usually become intrigued with increasing their hanging time. If the teacher cannot be available personally to supervise in a large class, perhaps an older child aide, or volunteer, could assume this important role.

Eventually, children will not need an adult's attention to enjoy hanging on a gym bar. Or, children may count for one another, perhaps using the gym bar as one station of a partner-type obstacle course. (See Obstacle Courses, p. 134.)

Variations:

1. Hang and swing; swing and drop; swing and jump from the chinning bar.
2. As able, children will benefit from moving across a horizontal (overhead) ladder, hand-"walking."
3. As strength improves, chinning may be introduced.
4. A large, long climbing rope, hung indoors and/or out, which has been knotted every two feet, is a great boon for improving grip strength.
5. A tire swing also encourages some hand exercise.

36. / Rodeo Rope Spinning

For:

Strength and coordination of shoulders, arms, hands and fingers.
Rhythmic sense.

Age: All ages.

Materials: An individual rope for each child (if possible). A wiffle ball to put on the end of the rope is desirable; and/or a few tails of crepe paper; and/or a bean bag to tie on the end. If jump ropes are used, these generally are cut seven to nine feet long. Shorter rope lengths may be used.

Directions: Discuss the meaning of the words *rodeo, bronco* and *lasso*; include such facts as you or the children can gather: that a rodeo is a cowboy "circus"; the various events that may be included, such as lassoing and tying a calf, riding a steer or unbroken horse (a bucking bronco), etc.

Give each child a jump rope that has been doubled. The child will hold the fuzzy ends, and there should be a wiffle ball at the middle fold. If the child spins the rope with even a minimum of speed, the wiffle ball will whistle.

For the young child or uncoordinated child who cannot spin the rope rhythmically, the teacher should take the child's hand in hers (his) and together spin the rope. Even if a child cannot spin the rope properly, if he continues to jiggle the rope around, he eventually will get into rhythm, probably sooner than you might think.

Variations:
1. The child should attempt to spin the rope in both clockwise and counterclockwise directions, with first the preferred and later, the non-preferred hand.
2. The child may spin two ropes (with wiffle balls) at once.
3. In place of the wiffle ball, tie about six or eight ten-inch strips of crepe paper onto the middle fold of the rope. When spun, the crepe paper will make a pleasant fluttering sound like birds' wings, and is visually fascinating to watch.
4. For extra strength building and/or a different kinesthetic experience, tie a bean bag or small weight onto the center fold of the rope in place of the wiffle ball.
5. Child may spin a rope and jump at the same time. (Child is not jumping over the rope.)
6. Child may spin one or two ropes in various positions, such as overhead or low like a lasso.
7. Using one rope (with wiffle ball, etc.), the child may pass the rope from hand to hand, moving it around the body (front to back to front, etc.).
8. Older children may combine (alternately) spinning a rope (no wiffle ball, etc.) with jumping over the rope. See books on physical education for elementary children, for a wide variety of stunts while jumping rope.

Rodeo Rope Spinning

Comments: There is almost never a need to urge children to attempt or continue practicing this game. The motivation is built in. The simple equipment itself encourages the child to spin the ball with grace, rhythm and speed. The combination of the loose, relaxed motion and the balanced control required will have a likely positive effect on the relaxed control and coordination needed in chalk and chalkboard, or pencil and paper control.

For maximum transfer, this game might be followed immediately by chalkboard or pencil and paper writing or pre-writing exercises. Children might be told, "See if you can remind your arms and hands to be loose, yet controlled, as they were for rope spinning. Let your arms and hands help your fingers," etc.

10.

Follow-the-Leader Games

One reason that children like follow-the-leader games is that they are fast-changing. One can't become bored. It is exhilarating, too, to be able to do a whole string of stunts.

Teachers like it because it also combines a variety of physical skills, and exercises full concentration.

37. / Indian Walk Through The Woods

The game develops:

Body strength, coordination, agility and balance.
Body awareness in a variety of positions.
Following of visual directions (imitation).
Attention span increase.
Brain control of body: mobilizing the body for many quick changes and transitions.

Age: All ages.

Materials: None.

Directions: The Indian chief (the teacher or a leader) walks around a circle of children, tapping them one at a time on the shoulder and saying, "Follow me (us)." When all the children are in a line, the chief takes them for a walk through

Indian Walk Through The Woods

the classroom (or playground) in absolute silence. As the leader walks, he puts his arms in various visible positions. Examples: arms outstretched; right arm up, left down; hands on head, hands on hips; arms flapping. He may add jumps, hops, turns, bends, even walking backwards or sideways, marching, etc. At the signal, "Everyone run home!" children break from the line and run back to their same starting spots in the circle without touching any person or furniture.

Variations: The line preferably should consist of five or six children. In a large class, there could be two or three leaders simultaneously. The line(s) could move through large or small equipment, as under a table, between chairs, stepping through a ladder, etc.

Comments: Put your good watchers at the end of the line if possible. Young children should do only arm movements at first. Add leg movements (jumps, etc.) as able.

38. / Thousand-Legged Worm

For:

> Rhythmic movement of hands, legs, body.
> Imitation of movement.
> Changing movements quickly.
> Paying attention.
> Locomotor patterns: walking, jumping, hopping, swaying, etc.

Age: For primary age children.

Materials: A tom-tom is helpful but not necessary. (The teacher may clap instead.)

> *The song*: (to the tune of "Polly-Wolly Doodle")
> Verse:
>> "Oh, tell me," said the thousand-legged worm,
>>> "Has anybody seen a leg of mine?
>
>> If it can't be found, I'll have to hop around,
>> On the other nine-hundred ninety-nine."
>
> Chorus:
>> Hop around; Hop around;
>>> On the other nine-hundred ninety-nine.
>
>> If it can't be found, I'll have to hop around,
>>> On the other nine-hundred ninety-nine.

Directions and variations: There are many minor skills to be practiced separately before putting the thousand-legged worm train together.

1. Children should learn to clap with the song's rhythm, seated.
2. Children should practice tapping foot seated and/or stamping foot standing in one place, and/or swaying while standing in one place.
3. Children should practice walking and moving around slowly (marching).
4. Children should practice doing simple arm movements to rhythm: one arm out, or one arm up; or one arm down, one arm on hip; one arm shake, etc.
5. When children are familiar with the song and its rhythm, they may start to build trains of children, holding onto one another's shoulders lightly with one or both hands. The trains sing, (a) while marching slowly anywhere in the room, and (b) while copying the leader's arm and/or foot patterns. Arm and foot patterns may be omitted if desired and just have children march in trains, or march alone. Keep trains short (three or four children) except for skilled older children.
6. Fancy variations: some adept or older children may add shuffles, kicks, jumps, hops, knee-bends, finger-snaps, or moving the train backwards.
7. At the sound of a whistle or tom-tom, leader goes to the rear of train and we have a new leader.

Comments: This is a rather difficult game to master, so settle for partial success. Remember, the average child is not able to beat rhythm consistently until around age six.

Thousand-Legged Worm

Young primary children may do a rather sloppy job of following rhythm and/or leader's movements, yet still may gain benefits from the game.

Some helpful hints:

1. For a child who cannot sway in rhythm, the teacher may hold child's shoulders firmly and rock with him or her for a while.
2. Children may rock on their own until they can rock with the beat; only then may they join a train.
3. Place a child with weak sense of rhythm next to a child who has a strong sense of rhythm.

39. / Punchinello

For:

Rhythmic coordination (matching movements to verbal signals).
Thinking up one's own motion for the group to copy.
Body awareness in various positions (imitation of movement).

Age: Kindergartners, pre-schoolers, some first graders.

Materials: None.

Directions: Children stand in a circle. Child #1 is chosen to be the first Punchinello and he or she goes into the center of the circle, while everyone sings. When the song asks, "What can you do, Punchinello, funny fellow?" Child #1 begins any simple motion, for example, raising and lowering arms, hopping on one foot, clapping, patting the head, or swinging one arm or leg. When the song says,

Punchinello

Punchinello

"We can do it too," all children imitate Punchinello's motion. When the song finishes, Child #1 quickly picks the next Punchinello, who takes Child #1's place in the center and prepares to start a new motion. The song should repeat almost continuously until six or seven children have had a turn. Then the teacher could make a note of who has *not* had a turn for the next day's game.

40. / Mirrors

For:

Right and left awareness (simple and/or complex).
Body awareness in various positions in space.
Moving slowly (inhibition and precise control of body parts).
Integrating visual and motor (kinesthetic) stimuli.

Age: Young children should be expected to *approximate* the leader's positions rather grossly. Older children may be expected to match the leader more precisely and change more promptly.

Materials: None.

Directions: There are many versions to this favorite game. Start by telling the class that it is a favorite exercise of dancers, and may be very easy or very complicated.

The teacher should be the leader (or mirror) first; later, children may take turns leading the group or one partner.

The teacher may say, "Pretend you are a mirror. Whatever movements I make, the mirror must reflect. If the leader puts an arm out to the right, you will put your arm out *to the left*, so that you will be an exact reflection." The leader may move any part of the body or the whole body at once. Start with moving a single

Mirrors

arm. Particularly with young children, the leader must be sure to give the mirror time to look, to think, and to match the leader's position.

When the children have mastered the basic idea of the game, the class may divide into pairs and first one child may take a turn leading, then the other. As children become adept, more complex actions may be added.

Variations: Couples may join hands with spread palms together; or they may *almost* touch, placing spread palms only one inch apart. Soft, slow music lends a richer dimension to the game.

Comments: The teacher may discuss right and left, just slightly above the level that the children are on. Remember that six is the average age for naming right and left correctly on the self; naming right and left on another person is much more difficult. However, children need many non-demanding experiences with right and left at early ages, in order to internalize this skill slowly.

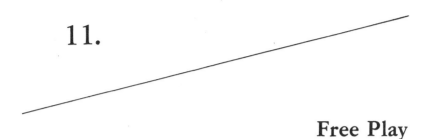

11.

Free Play

Reams have been written about the value of free play, and it's all true. However, I'm talking about a sort of semi-structured free play, where a special versatile item (or set) of equipment is put into the classroom for only a week or two at a time for children to explore in various ways. After the children have had a chance to play with the equipment in *their* ways, the teacher might suggest some additional ways to use it. The teacher might get on the equipment and play *with* them, following, leading, watching silently, or stimulating language.

The joy of using a toy creatively in ten different ways is an incredible morale and confidence builder. Also a vast amount of comparative sensory and language information is added to the "bank," and motor skills are developed.

41. / Boards And Trestles

The game develops:

> Experimentation, problem-solving, planning, self-testing.
> Imagination and creativity.
> Vocabulary of position, space, etc.
> Body awareness and space-judging.
> Balance and coordination.

Age: All ages.

Materials: One or two long boards (8 to 10 feet); one or two shorter boards (6 to 7 feet); two to four trestles (saw-horses), 2 high, 2 low.

bouncing board

slide & escalator

series of balance beams

Boards And Trestles

Directions: Children can arrange the boards and trestles fairly quickly into a variety of play equipment. It's interesting to see what they come up with.

Some possibilities:

High or low incline(s) to run, hop, jump, crawl, or slide up and down; head first, on stomach or back, etc.

A low or high diving board to jump from in various ways: far, near, spin-around, backwards, sideways, etc.

A see-saw; a bridge to roll or "swim" under.

A sequence of low and high balance beams to move along in various ways; on stomach, back; seated, straddling.

A jump board: one child might jump while others stand or sit on the board and feel the vibrations.

Various combinations of the above.

Imaginary objects: house, truck, scaffolds, etc.

Comments: Of all indoor, large-muscle equipment, boards and trestles are perhaps the most versatile, provide the widest range of physical activity, are the easiest to buy or make, and certainly grasp and hold children's attention for long periods of time.

42. / Barrels

For:

Space and size concepts.
Body awareness in various positions and spaces.
Balance and rhythmic coordination of whole body.
Hand strength.
Social skills. (In several activities, children must put their barrels together and work together.)

These activities are joyful confidence builders, therefore especially good for the withdrawn, fearful child or the non-expressive child.

Age: All ages. Young children may not be able to do all activities.

Materials: A set of barrels (open-ended and preferably nesting)—preferably four. If there are four barrels, children should work in groups of four. Barrels are available through school supply catalogues (expensive) or often for free through soap or other manufacturing companies.

Dimensions suggested: barrel diameters of about 17″, 21″, 23″, 26″; however, any will do that are large enough for a child to roll in. Even one barrel is useful, but versatility and fun are much increased if you have several.

Barrels

Directions (roughly in order of difficulty although all are easy):

1. Pop Goes the Weasel: children scrunch down in barrel, come up simultaneously with "Pop!"
2. Climbing in and out, tipping over: children may figure out various ways of getting in and out including lifting self by arms; climbing with a chair; soft-tipping barrel over by stooping down inside and over-it-goes.
3. Rolling in barrel:
   a. Child lies in barrel like a log; keeps fingers away from edge. As he turns, barrel will turn. May roll over a mat or other flat obstacles, or down a small incline.

      b. Hands and knees roll.

      c. Somersault: child stoops in barrel, crosswise, with head near toes.

4. Horse riding: child straddles top of barrel, rocks from one foot to other.

5. Over the top: child lies crosswise on top of barrel, rolls over and slides off or puts head on floor and turns somersault off.

6. Tiger tunnel: put barrels end to end along wall, crawl through frontwards or backwards.

7. Walk in the barrel: hold barrel up from the feet by a good grip on top edge.

8. Imaginative games: it's a trash can, a house, a car, etc.

9. Roller-coaster: the most hilarious game of all—several barrels are needed. Line up several barrels, crossways. (See illustration.) Child lies across first barrel and pushes off, rolls to second barrel, third, fourth, and slides off or turns somersault off. Two children or even three may ride simultaneously if they are careful when sliding off.

Comments: Barrels are very stimulating (physically and mentally), and generally an aide or teacher should be present to direct traffic and prevent bumps. Ideas and squeals of delight flow freely in the barrel corner. It also follows that children may become overstimulated so a total barrel time of not more than fifteen minutes is suggested. Warn children three minutes before termination that it soon will be time to stop and move to another (quiet) activity. The time and trouble it takes to supervise barrel play is repaid many times over in terms of the skills and confidence that the children develop.

    It *is* a chore for a busy teacher to locate a source of free barrels. Perhaps a kind parent would take on this job.

43. / Inner Tubes

For:

Discovery and improvising: making up one's own activities.
Body awareness in various planes and positions.
Agility, balance, spatial relations.
Language stimulation.

Age: All ages.

Materials: Several inflated inner tubes (generally available at service stations or tire stores). Children may play in small groups so that each child has a tire tube.

Directions: It is suggested that this activity be started out by presenting several children with an inner tube each, with little or no comment, and with the teacher watching unobtrusively and monitoring traffic. Allow the children to figure out

Inner Tubes

ways to use the tubes. When and if children are unable to think of further activities, the teacher may offer suggestions in a non-demanding way. All ideas should be praised.

Variations: Some possibilities that have been thought up by children include these:

1. Jump in, on, or over, one or a row of tubes. Combine tires with hoops or rope circles to make an obstacle course.
2. Bounce or straddle folded tube, horse-style.
3. Roll in, in various ways.
4. Crawl through, without touching tube.
5. Roll tube like a hoop, either while walking beside it, or roll it fast to another person. Walk it along a balance beam or string line. Roll it fast so that it bounces over a low balance beam or board.
6. Somersaults: place head on one side of tube, somersault over to other side. Tube is at rest on floor.
7. Sitting in tube, stretch legs out straight to make a "boat"; then rock, scoot, or tip the boat.
8. Use tubes as targets for bean bag toss.
9. Imaginative play: birds in a nest; carry tube at waist height for a "space ship."
10. Language stimulation: at any point, the teacher may stimulate, in an unobtrusive way, the language of body parts, positions, spatial arrangement, etc. by (a) feeding in descriptions of what a given child is doing, for example, "You're really fitting your whole self into a small space"; or (b)

by asking the child to put into words what he or she is doing, as "Can you tell me how you get the inner tube to roll so fast?"

11. Creative confidence: children will be quite noticeably stimulated by the teacher's positive reinforcement of any and all creative efforts, for example, "I like the way you're rolling in that tube. It reminds me of the story of the three pigs rolling down the hill in a churn."

Comments: Inner tubes are a most useful, versatile, and creatively stimulating toy. When children tire of them, as of course they will, put them out of sight for a few weeks.

44. / Rocking Boat

For:

Rhythmic coordination and balance.
Creative and cooperative play in a small group.
Language stimulation.

Age: Pre-school and kindergarten.

Materials: Sturdy rocking boats are available through all school catalogues. These can generally be turned upside down to make steps and a platform.

Directions and variations: Just bring a rocking boat and two, three or four children together. Allow children to use the boat in any (safe) way they want. If and when interest wanes, the teacher might suggest any of the following activities:

1. Rock and sing: "Row, Row, Row Your Boat"; it fits the rhythm of the rocking boat.
2. Alternate rocking and "swimming": "Pretend you're traveling down the Amazon River to collect water animals for the zoo. After each mile of travel, let's all get out, swim around, and bring back to the boat . . . let's see, what animal that lives in (or near) the water should we collect?" (all kinds of fish, alligators, frogs, water birds, snakes, etc.).
3. "Pretend our boat is a motor boat that we must buy gas for and start the motor by turning a key, pulling a string, etc."
4. "See this dock here? (a balance beam). When you get in or out of the boat, you're supposed to walk along the dock."
5. "Sit backwards on the edge of the boat and see if you can make it go."

Rocking Boat

6. "Turn the boat over, jump from the top step; walk up and down with eyes closed, etc."
7. "Pretend the top of the steps is a stage and you're doing a tap dance, etc."
8. "Turn the boat on its side and pretend the interior is a cave, etc."

12.

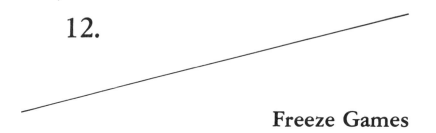

Freeze Games

I'll bet the children of the cave men played at quick stops and starts, so universal is this simple pleasure.

If the teacher says, "Hold still a moment," it seems like an imposition for many children. If a whistle says it, or a tom-tom, or even if Simon says, it's easy.

After hyperactive children have "frozen," a few dozen (or a few hundred) times, they often become convinced that their brains indeed have some say in what their bodies do.

45. / Red Light, Green Light

The game develops:

The ability to inhibit the body appropriately: stop and start.

Leg strength, agility, balance, coordination.

Quick reaction to auditory, verbal, or visual signals (listening and maintaining attention).

Age: All ages, with varying standards of performance expected according to age.

Materials: A tom-tom for the auditory version of the game. A spoon and pan will do.

For the visual version, three colored traffic lights (crayoned circles are fine), one red, one yellow, one green. Add a blue if desired.

Red Light, Green Light

Directions: Children run lightly on the word "green," walk on "yellow," and freeze on "red." (Skip or gallop on "blue" if children are five or six and up.)

Substitute a fast beat of tom-tom for run, a slow beat for walk, a loud thump for freeze. A brushing stroke of the tom-tom may be added for gallop or skip.

Substitute colored circles: green means "run," yellow means "walk," and red means "freeze" (blue for "skip" or "gallop").

Anyone who bumps into furniture or another person must lose a (short) turn, or sit in the resting chair.

Comments: See also Space Walk, p. 111.

46. / Catching Fish

For:

Body awareness in various types of space.

Listening and quick reaction: reacting to auditory signals and directions; changing locomotor patterns (walk, run, hop, etc.); changing body positions (touch toes, etc.).

Body strength, awareness, flexibility and agility.

Balancing and dodging.

Vocabulary of body parts, speeds, directions.

Social skills: getting caught (adds an element of suspense, but does not mean dropping out of the game; see comments regarding competition).

Catching Fish

Age: All ages.

Materials: A long string or rope or other divider (chalk line, etc.). A tom-tom (or whistle; a pan and spoon will do).

Directions: Divide the room in half with a rope tied to two chairs. Children all stand in one half of the room (the river—the other half of the room is the pond).

Story. The teacher or leader is the farmer who wants to add fish to his pond to stock it, so he goes to the river to see how many fish he can bring home. The farmer gives the fish (children) various directions how to move around their area (the river). When the tom-tom thumps hard, children *stoop* and *freeze*. The last one (or two) down get(s) caught, and must crawl under the rope to the other half of the room (the pond) where they continue to follow directions. The very last one or two children to get caught are today's winners. (Play down the winning aspect.) Play up the idea (as usual) that everyone who plays the game wins because "you're teaching your body how to react quickly in various ways."

Sample ways of moving: "When the tom-tom rattles, everyone walk forward with giant steps. Remember, no touching of other children or furniture or the rope, or you're caught."

For speeds, patterns, directionality: walk backwards, walk sideways (step-slide or cross over one foot), walk heel to toe, baby steps, etc., walk tip-toe, run tip-toe, skip, hop, jump or gallop frontwards, backwards, sideways. (Commands may be given separately for young children or combined for older ones, like walking backward, heel to toe, slowly.)

For body awareness, right and left: hands on head, hands on knees, hands on toes, hands on back, etc., right hand on left ear, left hand on right elbow, right hand on left knee, left hand on right knee, etc.

Comments: This clever, sneaky game was dreamed up especially to combine many important skills in a very slightly competitive context. There are two important values to competition (as well as several obvious defects if overdone):

1. A slightly competitive game holds the children's interest while doing rather routine practice of common skills: running, jumping, balancing, touching body parts.
2. It teaches children (hopefully) that "getting caught" is part of the fun of the game and that, in this game and in many of the games in this book, getting caught does not mean dropping out but merely changing roles. Briefly discuss "getting caught" with your children occasionally: (1) what it means and why we do it (to add interest to the game, *not* to judge who's best); and (2) how you feel when you're caught (hopefully *not* disappointed in yourself). Even small children sense the intent of this message.

The value of a story line: A story, such as "the farmer wants to catch fish to stock his pond from the river," makes a better game than "Now children, we're going to change from this space to that space." Teachers, add a story to any routine skill your children need to practice and presto, you have a game, you have their cooperation, you have added motivation, and you have achieved your goal of increasing children's skills. Let your imagination run rampant. (See Creative and Imaginative Play, p. 49.)

47. / Magazine Statues

For:

Body awareness in various positions.
Space-judging.
Right and left awareness and discrimination.
Language of body parts and position.
Integrating visual-verbal-motor stimuli.

Age: Young children may execute the various positions in an approximate way. Older children may be expected to be more discriminating, for example, in matching facial expression, finger positions, and/or correct left and right positions.

Materials: A set of six or eight magazine pictures of people in various standing or seated positions. The pictures should be stapled or glued to cards or cardboard for

Magazine Statues

easy handling. For young children, the pictures may be quite different; for older children, there might be similarities among pictures to require more refined discrimination.

Directions: The teacher shows the pictures to the children, discussing how they are alike and how they are different. Then he or she says, "Now the class will turn around and face the wall; no peeking while I arrange the first statue (Child #1) to be exactly like one of the pictures. The statue will freeze and hold in one of these (picture) positions. When the statue is ready, I'll say 'Turn and look.' Turn around and look carefully at it, but don't say anything. Then I will show you each picture in turn. When you think you've spotted the picture that our statue is acting out, raise your hand. Now, is it this one? (Hold up picture #1), etc."

Comments: The teacher should emphasize that each child in the audience should do his or her best to discriminate what is alike in the statue and in the picture. An important side benefit of this game is helping children think and decide for themselves. "Vote for the picture that *you* think is correct, not necessarily the one other children are voting for. If you decide on the wrong one, it doesn't matter." This is a good game to teach that a "wrong" guess can be as useful, in terms of learning, as a "right" guess.

48. / Spinning Statues

For:

> Balance, body awareness in various positions and spatial planes, and holding the body immobile.
> Creating an original statue position.

Spinning Statues

Age: All ages.

Materials: None.

Directions: The teacher and a child hold each other's hands, and lean slightly apart. (After the game is demonstrated, two children can be partners.) Gradually the two partners spin around and at a signal, "Ready, Set, Let go!" the pair drops hands; the child who is released takes several steps, quickly assumes any interesting pose, and holds it while other children watch and perhaps applaud. Several pairs could swing at once, if desired. It would be helpful for the development of body awareness and language if the teacher could comment on as many of the statue positions as possible, for example, "Look how Janie's right arm is stretched up high and her left arm is very low."

After the basic game is familiar, the teacher may say, "This time we're going to have the statues freeze into a happy pose" (or sad, angry, shy, afraid, funny, etc.; or a king, a clown, a bird, a tiger, etc.). For older children, the type of pose may not be called until the moment of release.

Comments: One big advantage to this game is that children almost certainly will use it at home and in the neighborhood. Some discussion of how to swing one's partner gently is suggested.

13.

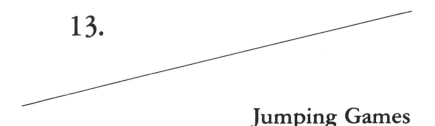

Jumping Games

Many children with learning problems lack the coordination to run or jump gracefully or without effort. They may fail to achieve minimal body strength and a vicious circle is set up with lack of strength contributing to an uncoordinated body, and uncoordination keeping the child largely immobilized and weak. Confidence suffers, and learning may be affected.

Sometimes a child has good body strength but he or she does not have the control to guide the feet and legs through a simple pattern.

Our running and jumping games involve two processes at once, one receptive, and one expressive: (1) taking in visual or auditory signals and (2) giving immediate commands to the body to follow what the signals say to do. The object is to program the brain to be in charge of the body. Later the brain can call its own signals and the body will respond.

49. / Animal Tracks

The game develops:

> Eye-foot coordination.
> Fitness and agility.
> Leg strength.
> Balance.
> Space judging.
> "Reading" visual signals and doing.

Age: All ages.

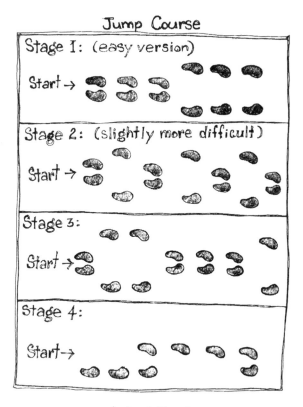

Animal Tracks

Materials: Masking tape, colored or plain; or chalk, or adhesive-backed shelf paper.

Directions: With masking tape (on a hard surface), or with chalk (on a carpet), place marks, to jump on, across the floor about one and one-half feet apart; use a very simple pattern for young children, increasing difficulty with age and/or ability. (See illustration.)

Variation: Cut footprints out of adhesive-backed paper. (See also Foot and Hand Prints, p. 176.) Children jump through the tracks that "an animal has left in the snow."

50. / Rope Jumping And Spinning

For:

Whole body endurance, agility and balance.

Whole body strength, especially legs.
Rhythmic coordination.
Visual tracking and coordination.

Age: Three to ten for spinning ropes; age six and older for jumping ropes. (Some adept younger children may jump rope.)

Materials: A long rope about twelve feet long. Short ropes seven to eight feet long (depending on age, and preferably one for each child). When purchasing *jump* rope, it is important that the rope be *sash cord* as this is heavy enough to provide a good rhythm, i.e., it turns well even in inexpert hands. Sash cord is much superior to clothesline or dime-store jump ropes. For other rope games, clothesline will do fine.

Directions: There are at least several good ways to teach rope activities.
1. Let the child practice *spinning* or *turning* both short and long ropes until the rhythm is familiar and internalized. Use either (and/or both) hands in both directions. This is a *very* valuable coordination skill in itself. Crepe paper strips, a wiffle ball, or a bean bag may be tied to short ropes to emphasize the feel, rhythm, beauty, and fun of the rope spin. (See Rodeo Rope Spinning, p. 77.)
2. Let child run through a long rope while it is turning. Turn rope toward child; he starts through as the rope hits the ground. Turning a long rope rhythmically is a valuable rhythmic coordinative exercise for eye-hand coordination.
3. Short rope: give each child a short rope. First let him spin the rope and jump beside it. Then, show him how to jump it in slow motion, first using the SSJT method: "*Slap* it in front of your feet, *stop* the rope there, *jump* over it, *turn* it over head and repeat." Eventually, he will speed up these operations. At some point let him experiment and "mess around" with the rope. I think it is useful to warn children it may take weeks or even months to get the hang of rhythmic jumps; but if they can manage to jump the rope even *once*, that is a successful start.
4. The carrot and stick technique: motivate children with fancy plastic-link jump ropes to be used, for example, when they can jump three, five or ten jumps in a row.
5. Trampoline: it is much easier to jump a long rope while jumping on the trampoline than on the ground because the trampoline provides the rhythm and lift. (A low pit-type trampoline is obviously easier here.)
6. Jump with chants, or numbers.

Comments: There are far too many perpetually tired children who gasp for air and give up at rather slight exertion. The culprit is not laziness or even poor

Rope Jumping And Spinning

attitude, but weak heart-lung strength. Rope jumping is one valuable way of counteracting poor endurance. Rope jumping (for boys, of course, as well as girls) is such a valuable skill, particularly for building heart-lung endurance and coordination, that many teachers include three or four minutes of it every day of the year as a warm-up before physical games or outdoor recess.

51. / Train Stations

For:

Practicing various types of locomotor patterns: hops, jumps, animal walks.
Balance, coordination, body awareness in various positions and spaces.
"Reading" a visual path.
Following auditory directions; stopping and starting on signal.
Attention and concentration.
Language development (especially categories).
Imaginative play.

Age: For younger children primarily. Stunts could be added to make a more challenging version.

Materials: A ball of string to represent the train track. Objects such as chairs, books, or sheets of paper to mark the stations. A tom-tom or whistle to signal the train to start is helpful but not necessary.

Directions: Unwind the string to form a path around the classroom. The string path may be straight, curved, may go through tunnels (tables), zig-zag around large furniture, etc. Each train station may be marked by a chair (or two) straddling the string. There may be many or few stations. Start with four or five, and assign one or two children to each station.

Take a little time to explain the direction of the trains. Have each child point to his or her next station to make sure each knows where to go and where to stop. "When you hear the tom-tom, the trains will begin to move. First we're going to pretend to be jumping trains; we'll jump along, straddling the string line until we get to the next station, where we'll stop and buy a sandwich." When children arrive at the first stop, let two or three children name the kinds of sandwiches that might be for sale, and all pretend to buy and eat. "All aboard now. Everybody point to the next station." The teacher can quickly see who may be confused as to direction, and help that child point to the correct spot. "This time we're going to hop on the right foot. Can you stand on your right foot? When you get to the station that you pointed to, rest a moment." At this stop, several other children name kinds of drinks (milk, orange juice, soda, etc.) and all pretend to buy and drink.

"Again, point to your next station. Good pointing. Now let's somersault along beside the track to your next station." At each stop children may rest, discuss, and act out familiar travel activities: buy a comic book or story book, take

Train Stations

a picture, visit a store, change clothes, etc. Between stations they may jump backwards or sideways; jump zig-zag along the track; take giant steps or baby steps; do jumping jacks; or animal crawls and walks.

Stop the game at any point *before* the children tire of it. The next time the game is played, perhaps the *children* could take turns deciding how they will move to the next station and what, if any, will be the activity during the rest stop. In short, change the game around any way you want.

Comments: The string will stick in place better if children straddle it rather than jump *on* it. (Masking tape could be used to help hold the string onto a tile floor.)

The entire game is, of course, an extremely legitimate device for involving children in practicing various jumps and other locomotor patterns, and in thinking about categories. It also illustrates the very important and useful technique of making the practice of routine skills more interesting by building a simple story around such practice. Imagination, language and memory are being stimulated as well. It makes no difference whatever whether the story is clever or not. Children are drawn to almost *any* story. Lucky teachers are not those with story-building talents, but rather those who experiment with making stories out of any ordinary idea that pops into their heads.

52. / Jump The Shot

For:

Tracking a ball.

Anticipating its approach (space and distance judgments), and mobilizing the body to jump over it at the appropriate moment (eye-body coordination).

Overall body strength and agility, particularly the legs.

Attention and quick reaction.

Age: Primary ages. Younger children can benefit from easier variations (Touch the Shot, Stop the Shot, Spin the Shot). Younger children also can practice Jump the Shot if considerable individual help is given, as in a very small group.

Materials: A rope about ten feet long, and any ball or small weighted object tied at one end, such as a bean bag wrapped in an old cloth, or an old deflated rubber ball. A tetherball works well but requires quite a high jump. A wiffle ball on a shorter rope can be used for Touch the Shot.

Jump The Shot

Directions: Children stand around the circumference of a large circle. The ball is swung in a large circle by a child or teacher standing in the center. The ball should skim along the ground or floor. As the ball approaches the children's feet, they jump over it. Any who are touched by the ball may receive some slight penalty, as one strike. Three strikes and you lose one turn.

Variations:
1. Touch the Shot: a lighter ball (as a wiffle ball) can be swung at shoulder height. As a child's name is called, he attempts to touch the ball with one forefinger as it approaches.
2. Stop the Shot: children sit in circle with knees drawn up. As the ball approaches, a child whose name is called reaches out with feet to touch or stop the ball.

Comments: Some teachers like to fasten a small solid rubber ball to the end of a fourth-inch diameter nylon rope, and tie the other end to a pole. This arrangement, while useful only for a smaller circle, is thought by some to be more easily maneuvered.

Even tired, heavy-footed children like Jump the Shot and will practice without complaining for longer periods than usual.

Some children who are otherwise bright and alert have such a poor sense of space and timing that they have no idea of when to jump, and fail to get ready as the ball approaches. Urging the child to jump more quickly does not always help. These children should have as much practice as possible in other, easier jumping games such as trampoline jumping, jumping over a slowly swaying rope, trying to catch and step on a "snake" (a rope that is being slowly dragged across the floor), and/or jumping over a rolled ball. Any easy pitch and catch game withbean bag, ball, or balloon will help also.

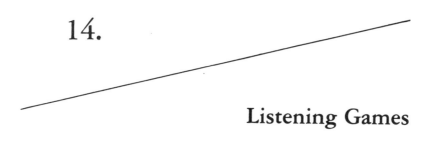

14.

Listening Games

Ask any teacher what is the single most important skill he or she would like a child to start school with, and chances are the teacher will say, "the ability to pay attention." Without the ability to really *hear* (and this does not refer to hearing acuity), the best teaching, the best lesson and the best intentions on the part of the student are wasted.

The ability to listen and understand are learned skills that many children pick up automatically. Legions of other children miss out. Listening games can help these children catch up, and can sharpen the senses of the adept ones.

53. / The Trolls And The Kids

The game develops:

Auditory skills: listening for, and freezing on signal.
Body control: inhibiting the body and changing pace, in a relaxed way.
Attention span.
Body awareness in various types of space.
Balance.
Vocabulary, especially words of position: over, under, high, low, through, in, out, around, up, down.

Age: All ages. Particularly useful for young children.

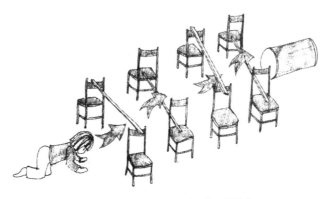

The Trolls And The Kids

Materials: A tom-tom (for the trolls). A "bridge" of four poles, broomsticks, or yardsticks, eight chairs and a barrel or table to crawl through or under.

Directions: A simple obstacle course is set up in the room (see illustration), consisting of two high poles and two low poles laid across the backs of eight chairs, perhaps with a barrel or table (for a tunnel) arranged near the last pole.

Tell a brief version of the story of the Billy Goats Gruff. Accuracy is unimportant. Explain the meaning of kids (young goats), for example, "Once upon a time there was a family of young goats (kids) who lived on a high mountain. They had to cross an old, rickety bridge to get to a field of grass for their food each day. Now under the bridge there lived some big, bad, make-believe trolls who liked to catch the young kids and take them to their cave. The kids learned to wait until the trolls went to sleep and started to snore before they crossed the bridge. Whenever the trolls would stop snoring for a moment to catch their breath, the goats would hold absolutely still. When the trolls started to snore again, the kids continued across the bridge. The kids became very skillful in stopping and starting because they listened very carefully for the trolls' snores," etc.

Children (the kids) are to step *over* the low poles and crawl *under* the high poles without touching them even slightly, and move through the barrel without a sound. If the poles rattle at all, those big bad trolls will wake up and grab the kids, and take them to their cave on the other side of the room (for one or two minutes only). The kids may only move when the tom-tom sounds a steady rumble (the trolls are snoring). When the tom-tom stops (the trolls are catching their breath), the kids must freeze, even if one foot is in mid-air.

The kids learn they must move quickly and silently to have more turns. The obstacle course may be elaborated in any way the teacher wishes.

Comments: This is one of the world's best games. Children never fail to fall in love with the Billy Goats Gruff tale set into three-dimensional reality. The tom-

tom and the danger of rattling the poles or barrel add just the right amount of suspense without being threatening. Children who ordinarily can't concentrate or hold still will freeze quietly and pay full attention to this game.

Little do they realize how rich the game is in educational skills.

54. / Robot Bowling

For:

Eye-hand coordination.
Figure-ground discrimination.
Waiting for and reacting to auditory signal.
"Reading" visual signals (words or pictures).
Social skills: fetching and carrying for classmates.
Following a series of events that together make the game go.
Extending attention span.

Age: Primary grades. Kindergartners can play with considerable direction. Six to eight children can play at once.

Materials: A set of ten-pins (wooden or improvised from milk cartons) and two rather heavy balls such as softballs or even volley or basketballs. A fifteen-foot plastic rug-runner (the alley) is desirable but not necessary; paper markers with labels, as shown in illustration.

Directions: For top view of the game, see Figure 54. Children move around alley counter-clockwise on tom-tom signal as follows:

Robot Child #1 bowls two rolls. (Optional: if she misses both times, she might get a third roll.) All the robots are programmed to freeze at their stations until the computer (the tom-tom) tells them, with a big thump, to move to the

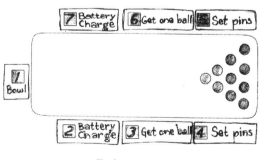

Robot Bowling

next station. Children move, robot-style, one station to their right. They then do what the paper sheet tells them to do and stand quietly at their stations while the next bowler rolls twice. Again, everyone waits for the tom-tom thump, then moves stiff-legged to the next station, etc. The game is ended when each child has had a turn at each station.

Comments: This game is a real winner that commands the attention and control of even hyperactive children for relatively extended periods.

The plastic rug-runner may be marked with ten dots to indicate where the bowling pins should be set.

55. / Pop! Goes The Weasel

For:

> Waiting for signal.
> Holding the body immobile.
> Synchronizing body action and verbal signal.
> Rhythm.

Age: Kindergartners and pre-schoolers.

Materials: None.

Directions: Children stoop in a circle, fingertips resting lightly on the floor for balance. Children sing the song, but it is prearranged that the teacher will sing the "Pop," and children know they must not jump up until they hear the teacher's "Pop." Sometimes the "Pop" comes immediately, sometimes children must wait three, five, even ten seconds before getting the "Pop" signal.

> *Words:*
> All around the cobbler's bench
> The monkey chased the weasel,
> The monkey thought 'twas all in fun,
> Pop! Goes the weasel.
> A penny for a spool of thread
> A penny for a needle,
> That's the way the money goes,
> Pop! Goes the weasel.

Variations: Children may play the game hiding behind chairs or in barrels.

Pop! Goes The Weasel

Comments: Even impatient children will hold still for many long seconds waiting for the right time to pop up. In fact, the longer they must wait, the better they
like the game. Praise children who wait for the "Pop!" Ignore any who pop up too
soon. If teacher puts finger to lips as he or she approaches the word "Pop," it will
remind children to hold and wait.

56. / Space Walk

For:

Learning the body parts and positions.
Balance and coordination: touching body parts while walking forward, side-
    ways, backward, etc.
Quick reaction to auditory signals.
Flexibility: physical and mental.
Space concepts.
Vocabulary development.
Left and right awareness.

Age: All ages. Incorporate more and faster changes for older children.

Materials: A tom-tom is very helpful, but not absolutely necessary.

Directions: "We're going to take a walk through space, changing directions,

Space Walk

positions and speed with verbal commands (and/or the tom-tom sounds, and/or colored paper traffic lights). Be sure not to touch any other person or furniture as you move around. Try to seek out the empty spaces of the room. Be careful when you go backwards—you may turn your head to look behind you." Keep commands very simple to start. Increase complexity very gradually.

Optional: Anyone who touches another person or furniture must drop out briefly.

Sample commands: "Let's walk forward with hands on hips—now hands on back, now hands on knees. Hobble along with hands on toes."

"Now go backwards with hands up in the air, now hands on ears, now on shoulders. Run lightly on tip-toes."

"Change and go sideways, with hands out to your sides. Now right hand on left knee and left hand on right knee."

"Let's walk as tall as we can; now bend down as low as you can."

"When the tom-tom thumps slowly, you walk slowly. When the tom-tom thumps one big thump, freeze quickly."

Optional: On the sound of a whistle, everyone stoops down. Last one (or two) down drops out. (See Catching Fish, p. 95.)

Comments: It's fun to watch a group of children start to loosen up and smile as they begin walking around the room in various positions. The child who is *listening* to the words of position while *watching* others move in the same *position he is in* is learning to integrate words with sensory information.

15.

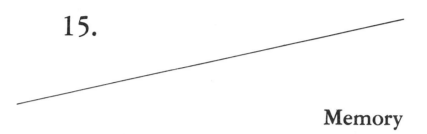

Memory

A large part of the thinking process depends on the *retention* of what is taken in, either for a short time (a few moments), or over a long term (several minutes, hours, days, weeks and months). A skill related to retention is *retrieval*: the appropriate selecting of what one has taken in and stored and producing what one needs.

Some people remember what has been *heard* very well; some remember what comes in *visually*. Many people can do both, many can do neither and many are erratic.

Memory can be a consciously strengthened operation for those who do not, for one reason or another, seem to come by it naturally. Strengthening memory through games, rather than through drills, does not remind a self-conscious child of whatever deficiencies he might have.

Whenever you are teaching memory games, discuss with children any and all memory techniques or tricks that they may use.

57. / Square-Circle-Diamond

The game develops:

Memory, through a variety of modalities: auditory, visual and kinesthetic.
Shape recognition and drawing.
Object-handling.
Eye-hand coordination.

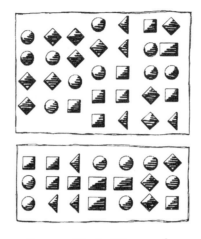

Square-Circle-Diamond

Age: Primary ages and kindergartners.

Materials:

Chalk and chalkboard, or pencil and paper.

Small cards to hold up as visual stimuli.

Three or four bean bags, and four or five templates or paper targets.

Directions: Auditory-verbal version. The teacher holds the chalk. Says to child, "Circle, circle, square." Child repeats this back to the teacher, "Circle, circle, square." If correct, teacher hands the chalk to the child and she draws circle, circle, square on the chalkboard. When she can handle three directions, add a fourth. If she cannot handle three items, use two.

Bean-bag auditory version. Teacher holds three bean bags, and gives the stimulus, "Circle, circle, square." If child repeats back correctly, teacher hands the child the bean bags which she throws at the proper targets on the floor: (a row of three, four, or five basic-shape templates, or three to five sheets of paper with the basic shapes drawn on them).

Visual version. Hold up a stimulus card which shows the three shapes: circle, circle, square, in a row. Put it down. Child repeats the stimulus pattern, "circle, circle, square." She then executes the pattern motorically by drawing or throwing bean bags at the shape targets. Patterns may be readily decreased or increased in difficulty.

58. / Command Cards

For:

Immediate, sequential memory.

Body awareness in various positions and spaces.

Vocabulary of body parts, positions and actions.

Command Cards

Age: All ages. Vary the tasks according to child's ability.

Materials: A set of eight or ten cards each having a different series of two, three, or four commands written on it. (Young children, three's, should start with two; older children may try three or four commands, or more.)

Directions: Each child takes a turn picking a card from the stack. Making sure the child is listening carefully, the teacher reads the commands (unless the older child can read his own). Put the card down. The child repeats the commands and finally does what the commands say. Commands may be very simple or very complex, depending on the age and ability of the child. Start easy, and add more tasks as each child is able.

    Examples: Turn around, then do a somersault.

                Jump, clap, touch your toes.

                Spin around once, hop, lie down.

                Balance on one foot, hop, stamp your foot.

Variations:

1. Child holds the cards. The teacher picks a card, reads it, and announces that he (the teacher) will follow the commands but will make a *mistake*. Children raise hands if they know what the mistake was.
2. Have some two-command cards, some three-command cards, some four and some five. Let child pick the kind he wants, easy or hard, etc.
3. Add some funny tasks (put your head under the chair, etc.); some strengthening or tumbling stunts (do a push-up, do a log-roll); have children help make up tasks.

Comments: Between turns, watchers are getting good memory practice checking the "doers."

59. / Echo

For:

Maintaining alertness.
Integrating and organizing input signals and motor output.

Age: All ages. The activity is easily adjusted to the capability of a single child. With practice the level of difficulty can be adjusted to a small group.

Materials: None, though the game may be played using tom-toms, wooden blocks or any simple instruments.

Introductory comments: The game appears very simple, and *is* for adults. The child (or children) attempts to duplicate exactly the clapping pattern given him by the teacher. In practice, as most teachers realize, the task involves many mental processes and is quite difficult for most children. Considerable thought and planning must precede the game to insure its success. There are so many benefits, however, that the game is worth considerable effort; and hopefully the teacher will put up with some trial and error. Every child can do the activity at some level. The trick is to find that level without asking too much too soon; and a greater trick is to cope with varying levels, as in a classroom group. The most common mistake is starting at too high a level.

Directions: Start with a single, slow-motion clap. There is a delightful little side-play that the teacher can use as a warmup, as follows: Everyone holds his arms out to the side, hands positioned ready to clap. The teacher says, "Now I'm going to try to trick you. I'm going to move my hands very, very slowly together. Now you move yours together too. All of a sudden I'm going to clap, and you see if you can clap immediately after I do. If you're watching very carefully, we'll clap *almost* together." This introductory game puts children in an attentive, alert mood for the more difficult tasks to follow.

Next the teacher may say, "Now listen carefully and see if you can match the exact number of claps I'm going to give you." Clap-pause-clap. The children echo clap-pause-clap. If there is a general mix-up, it may be necessary to have children take turns individually or in groups of two or three. If all children can do clap-

Echo

pause-clap, the teacher may slowly move to more complex patterns as CLAP (loud)-clap (soft); CLAP, CLAP, CLAP, clap; CLAP, CLAP-pause-clap, clap; etc.

Variations:

1. Older and adept children may not only do increasingly complex patterns, but also may transpose the claps to written symbols: loud claps become dashes; soft claps become dots.

2. They also may take turns transposing written symbols that the teacher flashes from cards into a sequence of claps.

3. Claps may be combined in any simple pattern with foot taps.

4. Simple *words* may be echoed using various combinations of fast-slow, loud-soft, pauses or whispers. Every day, the teacher may say "Good-bye" in a different tone of voice, which the children might echo. Nonsense words might be echoed, or a short sentence as "Let's (pause) go outside (pause) now." Older children may attempt long sentences.

5. Two or three words may be said backwards.

6. A series of numbers might be echoed forward or backwards.

7. To practice delayed memory skills: even a few seconds delay in repeating back a pattern, particularly if that pattern has no intrinsic meaning (as a series of taps or claps), is difficult for many children. Therefore, to increase awareness and strength of this skill, the teacher might (a) present any of the above clapping, word or number patterns, (b) silently count to three, five or ten, and (c) *then* signal the child to try to repeat the pattern exactly.

60. / Concentration

For:

Visual memory, spatial organization.
Matching number or picture cards.
Finger dexterity.

Age: All ages. Young children can play a simplified version of the game by using fewer pairs of cards. Two to six persons may play at once. With young children, benefits will be greater if only one or two children play with an adult who provides assistance.

Materials: A deck of cards.

Directions: The cards are turned face down on a table, either in rows or helter-skelter. (For the first game only, or with young children, it is suggested that only face cards be used.) The object of the game is to match and save pairs. Each player, in turn, turns up two cards. If they are of the same number (or picture), the child keeps them and takes another turn. If they do not match, the two cards are replaced face down and the turn passes. The players soon realize that they can remember the location of many cards turned up by themselves or the other players so that when their turn comes again, they may readily make one or more pairs. Continue until all cards have been paired. The winner is the person who takes the most pairs.

Concentration

Comments: The teacher can assist a child who is having trouble remembering the location of cards by suggesting memory techniques. For example, the teacher may verbalize aloud how he or she remembers the location of cards as, "I'm going to try to remember that the King is in the corner, and there's a six next to it."

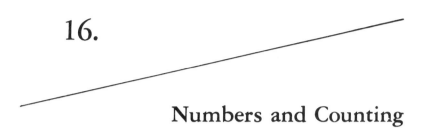

16.

Numbers and Counting

Of the many aspects of number concepts, counting intangible things is an incredibly difficult task for most children. If you say "Jump four times in this hoop," the child might jump two times while carefully counting to four, and be absolutely sure he has jumped four times. In counting the number of ball bounces, children become confused quickly. The games which follow provide an enjoyable means of matching actual jumps or bounces with verbal counting.

Although children under age six or seven may not be able to absorb fully the number concepts involved, the experience of attempting to count jumps, bounces, motions or spaces is a valuable supplement to the counting of concrete objects. If the teacher does not press young children for correct answers, each child will take from the games whatever is appropriate for him or her.

61. / The Mouse And The Cage

The game develops:

> Eye-hand coordination; more intricate space judgments and timing.
> Object handling.
> Counting (should be omitted until motor parts are mastered).

Age: Five or six and up for counting practice; four and up without counting.

Materials: A ping-pong ball and small (foil) pan for each child.

Directions: It is suggested that this game be practiced in very small groups so

The Mouse And The Cage

the teacher can give much help in getting started. The ping-pong ball is the mouse, and the pan is the cage.

The idea is to drop the ping-pong ball, let it bounce once, and catch it in the pan with the other hand. Next, let the ball bounce twice and catch it; three times, etc. Four-year-olds should not be expected to go beyond three or four bounces, even without counting.

Many children tend to throw the ball down or to come in with the pan too late. Teach such children each part separately by saying, "I'll be the mouse, and you be the cage. See—I'm letting the ball fall out of my fingers from about this height (eight to ten inches). After it bounces you try to catch it in your pan." Practice several times.

"Now, I'll be the cage and you be the mouse. Watch how I slide the pan under the ball and raise the pan just a little as the ball falls in." (Repeat several times.) "Now you try both."

Comments: This is one of those games that is "easy once you know how." The delicate movements required are somehow not frustrating, probably because the game is a motivating one.

62. / Hoop-Hop

For:

> Counting while jumping.
> Strength, agility, balance and coordination.
> Matching visual, auditory and kinesthetic information to an intellectual, symbolic concept.

Age: Primary grades. Younger children will benefit from practice of a simplified version.

Hoop-Hop

Materials: Hula-Hoops or rope or chalk circles placed in a row. Always start on the left; move to right. This game could be one section of an obstacle course.

Directions: Demonstrate the jumps and counts. Discuss how hard it is to keep the jumps and counts together.

The child walks into the first hoop and jumps once while counting "one" aloud. Then he *walks* into the second hoop and jumps twice, "One, two." Then he walks into the third hoop, jumps three times, etc.

Comments: It sounds so easy and *is*, from an adult point of view. The teacher should supervise the jumps closely at first, giving help as needed and settling for an imperfect match of jumps and counts from some children.

63. / Ten Little Indians

For:

Learning to count to ten, forward and/or backward.
Concrete experience with, and acting out, numbers.
Associating number actions, number words and written symbols.
Finger dexterity and coordination.

Age: Primary grades, kindergarten; pre-schoolers may do the first version slowly. However, any number learning for them will probably be rote (still useful).

Ten Little Indians

Materials: In versions one and three, none; large cards or sheets of paper with numbers for version two.

Directions:

Version 1. Practice raising the fingers one at a time without music. Next, the "Ten Little Indian" song can be sung, as slowly as needed, so that children can raise fingers one at a time as the appropriate number is sung. When children have mastered counting upwards, children then may practice lowering fingers one at a time, first without music and later to a slow-motion version of the song, "Ten Little, nine little, eight little Indians."

Version 2. Give each of ten children a sheet of paper with one of the numbers from one to ten on it, and let them stand in front of the class in order. As the song is sung, each child, in number order, takes a large step forward (or children may rise from seated to standing position as their number is sung). When this is mastered, children might step backward one step as the song is sung "in reverse."

Version 3. Children repeat version 2 without the visual assistance of the numbered sheets of paper.

Comments: Don't forget to sing "Ten Little Indian Girls" at least half the time.

64. / Ladder Play

For:

Whole body experiences with numbers in series.
Sequential memory.

Balance, leg strength and agility.

Transposing word problems, or symbol problems, into actions and vice versa.

Age: For primary grades; pre-schoolers can do Version 1.

Materials: A ladder, placed on the floor; 3 ∧ 5 cards and masking tape. If no ladder is available, one can be "drawn" on the floor with masking tape.

Ladder Play

Directions: There are many excellent activities to be done on a ladder, with or without adding the number and counting element:

Version 1 (activities without numbers).

Walk through, run through, jump through:

with two feet into each square,

with one foot into each square,

with one foot inside the square, and other foot outside the ladder.

Jump into alternate squares.

Move forward, sideways, or carefully, backwards.

Walk rungs only; walk rails only.

Raise ladder on secure blocks, and repeat above activities.

Combine above with batting; for example, hit the ball, run to first base through the ladder. (See also Hit-and-Run Dodge Ball, p. 80.)

Raise ladder higher, and crawl over and under rungs.

Version 2 (activities with numbers). Mark each ladder square with a numbered 3 × 5 card, taped on. Type some simple tasks onto other 3 × 5 cards, which children can select from a pile. Of course, the teacher may read cards and give help in explaining. Tasks could be "singles": "Take eight jumps forward," double tasks: "Walk to five, then jump to ten," or triple tasks: "Walk to three, jump to six, throw bean bag to nine."

Version 3 (addition and subtraction). Some primary age children might jump out addition or subtraction problems:

"Jump to six, then jump two more. Where are you?" (Eight).

"Walk to nine, walk backward to start. Write your answer on the board."
   (Zero).

"Walk to six, walk back two. What's your answer?" (Four).

"Look at this equation on the card: $5 + 3 = 8$. See if you can jump it."
   (Jump to five, pause, jump three more, stop on eight.)

"Look at this problem on the card: $2 + 3 = ?$ See if you can jump to the
   answer. Count as you go."

Comments: Although children certainly can learn while watching their classmates take turns in this game, it is suggested that the class be divided into small
groups for ladder play. A group could be further divided into teams, and points
recorded for correct addition and subtraction problems. A few of the above activities could be played on an overhead ladder, for example, hand "walking"
forward and backward a given number of spaces.

17.

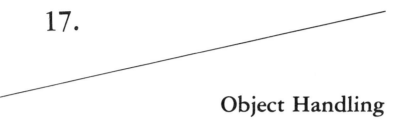

Object Handling
(and Ball Activities)

The skills of grasp, handling, and release are used without thinking, many times each day, for example, when we pick up a pencil, put on our glasses, dial the phone, turn on a faucet. We adults take these simple abilities so much for granted that we forget they must be learned over a period of years in childhood. The many children with small muscle coordination problems seem to have an especially difficult time. Imagine the frustration children who cannot even catch a large ball must feel when they are expected to print letters and numbers legibly. Also, many social games depend on picking up, handling, throwing, or catching objects.

Our eyes, too, grasp, manipulate and release letters and words during reading. Some psychologists feel that object-handling games have a positive effect on the refined type of eye muscle control required in reading.

65. / Bean Bag Activities
(Self-toss)

The game develops:

> Smooth, rhythmic grasp; manipulation and release of objects and visual steering of hands.
> Space judgment and timing.
> A feel for direction.

The vocabulary of direction and space:

above-below	back-forth	inside-outside
high-low	up-down	apart-together

Single-handed action (unilateral); two-handed action (bilateral).

Age: All ages.

Materials: One bean bag per child.

Directions: Many young children (and many older ones) find it difficult to throw with accurate aim, or to catch from a classmate. Therefore, we will concentrate first on self-tossing activities. Children sit on the floor with legs crossed or circled to form a "boat." To keep children from acting silly with the bean bag, say "Pretend you're a boat and there's water all around. Keep your bean bag in your boat (within the leg circle). Don't let your bean bag get wet, or we may have to hang it up to dry awhile."

Activities roughly in order of difficulty:

1. Popcorn: "Put your hands together, little fingers touching and pretend you've made a skillet. The bean bag is the popcorn. The skillet is heating up, and the popcorn begins to pop. Let it (the bean bag) move up in little pops, but don't let it fall out of the skillet." Gradually increase the height of the toss.

2. Pouring milk: "Hold one hand, with the bean bag, up high. Hold the other hand exactly under it. Start with hands about eight inches apart, increasing distance as you are able. Pretend you're pouring milk (the bean bag) from one pitcher to another. Reverse hands and pour the milk again. *Watch the bean bag with your eyes* to make sure you are aiming correctly."

3. Flapjacks: "Pretend your two open hands are two small skillets. You're

Bean Bag Activities (Self-toss)

tossing a flapjack pancake from one to the other, side to side." Widen the distance as able.

4. Single hand toss: "Let right hand only be the skillet; let the bean bag pop up a small distance (three or four inches)." Gradually increase height; then use left hand only.

5. Elementary aim: "Hold the bean bag up as high as you can and see if you can drop it in your boat (the circle of your legs), exactly in the center, without it touching you or your clothing."

6. Drop and clap: "Hold the bean bag high as in (5). Get your other hand up high too. Drop the bean bag and clap once as it falls." Don't worry if the child must clap *after* the bean bag hits the floor.

7. Eventually children may work up to clapping while tossing and catching the bean bag, but for little children this may take many weeks or months.

Comments: Try all the activities standing, and/or seated on a chair.

Many children must be reminded that to aim correctly, they should look at the bean bag before, during and after the toss.

Children should have opportunities during free time to experiment with and toss the bean bags any way they like.

66. / Scoops And Wiffle Balls

For:

Eye-hand-body coordination.
Social skills: working with a partner, accepting own and partner's goofs, and sportsmanship.

Age: All ages.

Materials: One scoop for each child; one wiffle ball per pair of children. To make scoops, just cut off the bottom of large, plastic milk cartons or bleach bottles with a knife. (Preferably use gallon size.)

Directions: Children face partners about six or eight feet apart. Show children how to hold scoop so edge is flat on floor and the ball can be rolled in easily.

Step 1. Child rolls ball by hand toward partner's scoop. Second child returns ball by hand-rolling to first child's scoop. Young children may stay at this level for several weeks.

Step 2. First child low-bounces ball to partner's scoop. Second child returns it the same way.

Scoops And Wiffle Balls

Step 3. First child low-bounces ball to partner's scoop, using his scoop to throw with instead of his hand. Second child returns it the same way.

Step 4. First child high-bounces ball to partner's scoop. Second child returns it.

Step 5. Child tosses own ball into air with scoop and catches own ball.

Step 6. First child throws ball from scoop to second child who catches it on the fly with a scoop. Only children age five and up should be expected to do this.

Variation: After children are past the rolling stage, a long rope down the center of the floor provides a good "net." Jump ropes laid across the center "net" give each child a court of his or her own.

Comments: At the beginning stages of partner ball-games, it is usually strategic to match an adept and/or patient child with an inadept and/or easily discouraged child. As children become more proficient, there should be opportunities for adept children to have equally matched partners.

Sportsmanship: Before starting the game it is good to discuss directly, "What will you say and what will you do if *you* make mistakes or *your partner* makes mistakes?" Children are sometimes poor sports simply because they have never been told exactly how to be a good sport. Role-playing or teacher demonstration of misthrows or miscatches is often helpful and fun.

67. / Easy Ball Activities

For:

Visual tracking.

Eye-hand coordination: grasp, handling and release of objects.

Concepts and language of space, size, distance, speed, time, direction and force.

Quick reactions.

Basic game skills.

Age: All ages generally need practice. Even two-year-olds can do some of these activities.

Easy Ball Activities

Materials: Several beach balls for a class (make sure ball rolls and bounces straight); a wiffle ball for each child; a box of assorted sizes of balls from a marble to a beach ball; and a plastic bat.

Directions:

1. Rolling. Young children should roll balls of all sizes often. Play hot potato ball using an assortment of various sized balls. Add a golf ball and a marble to the collection. (See Hot Potato Ball, p. 150.)

2. Balloons, Bean Bags. Next introduce Balloon play (self-tapping, or partner tapping back and forth) and easy self-toss bean bag activities. Make a skillet with both hands, let the bean bag pop like popcorn; "pour" the bean bag from one hand to another, from a height or side to side; sit with legs circled and drop the bean bag into the circle; touch the body parts

with the bean bag; balance the bean bag on head, shoulder, foot, etc. (See other Balloon and Bean Bag Games, pp. 125, 131.)

3. Wiffle Balls.
   a. After the child is acquainted with bean bag self-toss activities, he may do many of the same things with a wiffle ball.
   b. Have child sit with legs apart, feet touching a wall. He may roll the wiffle ball against the wall and it will roll back. Gradually, he can scoot back a few inches at a time and continue to roll and catch.
   c. Bouncing: sitting close to the wall, legs apart, child may toss the wiffle ball against the wall, at a height of twenty inches or so, and let it bounce back to him; he may scoot back as he is able to control the ball.

4. Beach Ball Activities.
   a. Roll ball to an adult and receive.
   b. Low-bounce ball to an adult, underhand, from three feet away.
   c. Hold ball overhead with both hands, push down hard and bounce ball to an adult; receive.
   d. Kick a ball to an adult. A hallway makes a good channel.
   e. Drop the ball and self-catch it.
   f. Toss the ball up (underhand), let bounce and catch.
   g. Overhead (and overhand) bounce a ball to an adult, counting several bounces.
   h. Dribbling: push down hard with both hands to get a short series of bounces. Much practice and experimentation is needed.
   i. Throw balls into boxes, baskets, hoops or any low or medium-high targets.
   j. Measure distance of throws with a rope or yardstick, or by marking the landing spot with a bean bag.

5. Batting.
   a. Suspend a wiffle ball with a rope from the ceiling. It should be about chest high. Hit the ball with hand, rolling pin, ping-pong racquet or plastic ball bat. (See Suspendable Ball, p. 199.)
   b. With plastic bat, hit a stationary ball from the floor or ground, golf-style.
   c. Hit a rolled ball.
   d. Hit a ball from a waist-high tee, pipe, post, or even a box.
   e. Finally, attempt to hit a slowly-pitched ball, thrown by an adult, from a close distance.

6. Easy Ball Games.
   Dodge ball.
   Kick ball and run to base.
   No-rules basketball. (Hoop must be low to insure success.)

No-rules ping-pong.

Hit wiffle ball or puck with hockey sticks and/or shuffle board sticks.

How Many Ways (can you move the ball)?

See how far you can throw.

Golf-baseball: bat ball from ground, run to base. (See also Hit-and-Run Dodge Ball, p. 152.)

68. / Nylon (Stocking) Racquets

For:

Eye-hand coordination.

Visual tracking.

Balance.

Whole body coordination.

Spatial judgment.

Figure-ground discrimination: the ability to concentrate on own balloon in spite of the distraction of other nearby moving objects.

Age: Easily varied to be challenging for any age.

Materials: Nylon racquets are very easy to make, requiring only about five minutes each; children can make them easily. A balloon for each two children will be needed, and a string or rope for a center line is helpful. To make the nylon bat, you will need a coathanger, a section of old nylon stocking or pantyhose; a rubber band or wire (plastic bag) tie. To make: pull the coathanger into a diamond shape, and stretch the nylon stocking over the coathanger. Fasten the stocking at the neck of coathanger with a wire tie or rubber band. Bend the hook of the coathanger into a closed loop—that's all. You may draw a face onto the racquet with a magic-marker if you wish.

Directions: With the racquet, children tap a balloon back and forth across a chalk or string line, which has been placed on the floor (or stretched high like a badminton net). Older children may keep score if they wish. To avoid collisions, children should be reminded not to step over the center line. Retrieve a balloon that falls into a neighbor's "court" by going behind neighboring players. Other than these courtesies, there need be no rules.

Variations:

1. For young children, an easy introduction to the use of nylon racquets and a good eye-hand coordination game in itself is to play "follow-the-string-golf." A rope or string-line may be zig-zagged around the classroom floor.

Nylon (Stocking) Racquets

Using the nylon bat like a golf club, children may lightly tap a newspaper ball or other small ball along the string path. Newspaper balls are made by crushing a sheet of newspaper and wrapping with masking or scotch tape.

2. Older children may experiment with hitting various types of balls, ping-pong, wiffle, etc., and may even *catch* the ball by using the nylon racquet like a scoop.

Comments: If the teacher wishes, a brief story may be told to the children as a lead-in (or motivator) prior to this game. Whenever possible, in all games, there should be some verbal interchange between teacher and children in which children may share some related experience. The objects are to increase language in general, to stimulate interest and to live the close relationship that exists between concrete action and the symbolizing of that action with words.

Again, the story need not be clever, funny or deeply "educational." *Any* story will capture the children's interest and will model language and creativity as well. As with homemade toys, children seem to appreciate homemade stories, and sense that such a story is a true gift.

Story: Once upon a time, in a dark basement of a large old house, there was a box of toys on a big, old, red bookshelf. In the box were a ball glove, a tennis racquet, some trucks, dolls and two table games: *Uncle Wiggly* and *Monopoly*. Every day the children who lived in the house came downstairs and got out some of the toys, and every evening the children put them back. Now, next to the box of toys there was a dusty box of junk. In this box were some old rusty coathangers, some ladies' old stockings with holes and runs in them, some plastic bag ties, some newspapers, some masking tape and some tired old balloons left over from a birthday party. The children never even looked at this box. All the things in the junk box were sad because no one ever played with them. One night they got an idea. The coathangers jumped out of the box and pulled themselves into diamond shapes, the old stockings stretched themselves over the diamond-shaped coathangers, and the little ties wrapped themselves around the stockings to hold them on. The newspapers first stretched themselves out and then crunched up into a tight ball, and the masking tape wrapped itself all around the paper ball. The balloons blew themselves up, but not too much. One did pop, however, and another balloon was cracked in its neck and had to sit out. All the new junk toys piled back into their box and waited. When the children came down the next day, they squealed with delight, "Look! New toys!" They took the new toys upstairs and played with them all that day and off and on for many days after that.

The junk toys lived happily ever after.

18.

Obstacle Course

An obstacle course can be a most valuable classroom management tool for teaching motor skills. Because it involves several stations, each child (in a small class) or each small group (in a large class) can be doing different activities simultaneously. On signal, children move from one station to another—this eliminates boredom, allows each child to work on a variety of skills in a short time, and provides the child with an abundance of sensory information with which to make comparisons. In my experience, any (easy) obstacle course is so interesting and so much fun that discipline problems are almost nonexistent.

69. / Improvised Obstacle Course

The game develops:

> Space judgment.
> Balance and coordination (especially eye-foot coordination).
> Agility.
> Response to visual signals.
> Comparative body awareness in various space situations.

Age: All ages.

Materials: Readily available objects from the classroom: chairs, tables, ropes or string, chalk, masking tape, large blocks, yardsticks, etc.

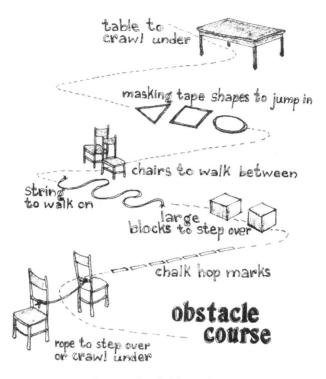

Improvised Obstacle Course

Directions: Arrange obstacles around the edge of room or in as large a circle as space permits.

1. Chairs placed about one foot apart for children to walk between without touching.
2. Chairs placed like ski flags to zig-zag around.
3. Chalk marks to jump over, across, or to use as footprints.
4. String or ropes arranged as straight, curved or zig-zag lines to walk beside, or as circles to jump into.
5. Masking tape hop marks; masking tape shapes to jump in.
6. Large blocks to step over without touching, or to step on like stepping stones.
7. Yardsticks to walk heel-to-toe or placed across chairs to crawl under, and/or step over.
8. Table as a tunnel.

Start children at various points on the course. In a large class, children could move in pairs or three's. Remind children that they should keep a safe distance between themselves and the children they follow. Optional: children may move to next station only on a tom-tom signal.

Variations:

1. When a tom-tom sounds, children freeze.
2. You may want to add some play equipment like a ball to bounce, a barrel or tin-can stilts, etc.
3. A course can be made outdoors with chalkmarks or heavy string connecting the apparatus in a sequence.
4. Animal walk pictures may be added to the obstacle course here and there.

Comments: Children may think up some obstacles the teacher may have missed. Any classroom contains abundant materials for an improvised obstacle course.

70. / Deck The Halls

For:

Practicing a wide variety of locomotor skills in a short distance and a brief time.

Utilizing transition or otherwise "dead" time to increase strength, coordination, balance, agility, body awareness and spatial judgment.

Increasing mental and psychological as well as physical flexibility.

Memory.

Reading visual signals (pictures or words).

Age: All ages.

Materials: Some large cards and gym tape (available at sporting goods stores). Masking tape would do.

Directions: Select a hallway that the children use frequently as a group. This may be the hall leading outside, or leading to the lunchroom or bathroom. If the classroom has no hallway long enough, set up the obstacle course in any frequently used traffic path within the room. The idea is to create a very easy obstacle "street," and whenever the children use this street (or at certain specified times), children do what the cards tell them.

Divide the hallway into sections by placing a strip of gym tape across the hall every six or eight feet. These indicate "traffic lights," where children stop and change to the next position. Hopefully, there will be room for many changes, perhaps as many as ten, but even two or three are much better than none. Next, on the wall beside each gym tape "traffic light" place a card indicating what kind of walk is required (sideways, backward, crossover); what kind of jump (forward, left side lead, right side lead, backward); what kind of hop (on left foot, on right foot);

Deck The Halls

or what kind of animal walk or stunt (pick easy ones—see Twenty Five Easy Stunts, and Animal Street). The card on the wall should illustrate the hop or jump with stick-figures as well as possible—it's not exactly easy to illustrate "hop on your left foot," but do the best you can. Include the appropriate words too, even though children may not be able to read. You will obtain more mileage from this obstacle course if the tasks are easy and require little supervision. Stairs are excellent for stretching the legs over two or three steps, and for pulling the body up via both hands on the bannister.

At least once a day, the teacher should remind children to use the path as an obstacle course. It is possible that children will use it for many weeks and even months; hopefully, it will become an automatic reaction. If the teacher indicates that he or she values the obstacle course, the children will too. If the teacher can take a moment each day to observe children on some part of the course and give positive feedback ("I see lots of good hoppers today"), interest will be maintained for a relatively long period. Should children become completely tired of the course, take the cards down, leave them down for a few weeks and put them up again in different order, and/or make new cards with new locomotor activities.

Variation: For sequential memory practice, at the halfway point of the obstacle course or at any point, stop the child or group, look back over the course, and say, "Can you name the hops and jumps we've done so far, in order?" Child will hopefully answer, "First we jumped forward, then sideways, then backward. Then we hopped on one foot." Some children will be able to name only one or two, some three or four. Few, if any, will be able to name all the jumps.

71. / Toy Shop

For:

Using the fingers and hands in a variety of contexts, for obtaining compara-
tive visual, tactile and kinesthetic feedback.
Stopping and starting on signal.
Tolerating the minor frustration of stopping in the middle of an activity.

Age: All ages. Young children may need considerable adult assistance, if some of
the toys are new to them. It is suggested that part of the toys be familiar.

Materials: A collection of fine motor toys or activities that may be sampled for
short periods, for example, pegboards with pegs and rubber bands; Play Dough
and molds; magic slate; large and/or small templates or dimestore stencils; small
chalkboard and chalk; cards (to sort or match); parquetry or other large or small
blocks with patterns appropriate to the age; sewing cards; yarn or string to draw
with on sandpaper; plasticene clay in a tray (see Clay Tray, p. 142); magnets; coins,
beans or clothes pins to drop in a jar; marbles to roll at a paper, plastic or cardboard
target; panball. A tom-tom or whistle, with which to give signals, is helpful.

Toy Shop

Directions: It is suggested that six or seven children visit the toy shop at one time, each child working alone at each of six or seven stations. It is possible to have two children at a station at once if there are duplicate toys. It is desirable to introduce the game with a brief discussion of toy stores and what fun it is to look at all the toys. "Wouldn't it be fun if you could play with all of them? In our toy store, you can, etc." Arrange the toys on table tops or on the floor, with some space between each and assign a child to each of the stations. Briefly demonstrate any new toys. Explain which way the circle will be moving on a signal. It is very important that the teacher explain that this game is like a "toy cafeteria," where the child will have just a few minutes to sample each toy; and when the signal is given (a tom-tom thump), he must stop even if he is not quite finished. Explain that at free time, the child will be allowed to pursue any of the toys he particularly likes, without interruption. If the toy shop rule is explained this way, children are *not* frustrated, and are quite willing to stop any activity and get ready to see what's coming next.

Each child works three or four minutes at his assigned station. Then the teacher sounds the tom-tom, which means "Stop, stand up, and point to the next station." The teacher can quickly determine if any child does not know where to go next, and give him help. When all children are pointing to the correct station, the teacher says, "Move to the next station and start with your new toy." After three, four or five minutes at this station, the tom-tom sounds again; and so it continues until the circuit is completed.

When the toy shop game is over, it is fun as well as good language and memory practice to discuss which toys were the favorites.

Even young children can stay with this activity for thirty or forty minutes.

72. / Health Club

For:

Strength, flexibility, balance and coordination.
Body awareness in various positions and spaces.
Starting and stopping on signal.
Self-confidence.

Age: Primary grades. Younger children will enjoy most of the items of equipment but will need more explanation and more help during the introductory stages.

Materials: Any combination of large or small gymnasium equipment, for example:

Dumbbells or junior bar-bells.

Health Club
Obstacle
   Course

Health Club

Any other light weights, as ankle or wrist weights, weighted jackets, etc.

An overhead ladder to hang on, a trapeze bar, etc.

A ladder on the floor to run or jump through.

Inner tubes or hoops to jump through.

Strings, ropes or poles to jump over or crawl under.

Balance beams, high or low; bounce-boards, twisters.

Boards and trestles.

Mats for doing a simple stunt or exercise on.

A stationary bicycle.

A slim-gym.

An elastic rope; a jump rope.

Bean bags and target.

A ball and a few bowling pins.

Directions: A large room is needed for this type of obstacle course—a gym or lunchroom. Arrange the stations around the room in any sequence.

If the children are familiar with the equipment, a larger group may use the "health club" at one time. If children are young or if some of the materials are new, it is best to arrange for only six or eight children to play at one time at six to eight different stations.

All equipment should be selected and arranged for maximum safety and a minimum of teacher supervision. An aide, a parent or older children as helpers are good but not absolutely necessary.

Before starting, the teacher should explain and/or demonstrate each piece of equipment briefly, emphasizing reasonable safety. Place one child (or more if desired) at each station; children will start to play on "go" and will freeze on the sound of a whistle or tom-tom signal. (Children will not be frustrated by this interruption, if it is explained to them ahead of time. See previous game, Toy Shop, p. 138.) After children freeze, each will point to the next station in the sequence. The teacher can quickly tell which children, if any, are confused about where to go next. When all children are pointing correctly, all children move to the next station and play for whatever time is appropriate (perhaps three to five minutes). And so the health club continues until all children have had a turn at each station, or until time or energy run out, whichever comes first.

Comments: An incredible variety of physical skills can be practiced, and a wide assortment of body awareness and space-relations experience can be added to the child's information bank. It is possible to continue the Health Club game on a semi-permanent basis for many days or even weeks by rotating out "stale" equipment and feeding in a few new items.

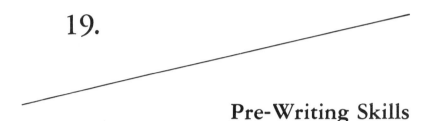

19.

Pre-Writing Skills

Reading really starts with readiness activities in the nursery. Writing also begins there with the control of certain hand and arm muscles, and with the visual awareness of scribbles, lines and marks made with crayon, chalk, pencil, paintbrush, a stick or a finger. Every marking experience, whether primitive or complex, adds to the visual-mental-verbal-physical information bank that culminates in the symbolic markings we call writing.

73. / Clay Tray

The game develops:

> Strength of the muscles needed for printing and handwriting.
> Eye-hand coordination.
> Shape recognition (perception).
> Small space awareness: directionality.

Age: All ages.

Materials: About four "butter-shaped" sticks of plasticene oil-based modeling clay, warmed in an old cookie tray in a slow oven, and spread evenly over the tray. The clay should be about 3/8 inch deep. An old blunt pencil or defunct ballpoint pen to draw with.

Directions: Older children may print or write in the clay with an old blunt

Clay Tray

pencil or pen. One really must push and pull to get the pencil to move through the clay; meanwhile, the hands grow strong.

Younger children can draw in the clay, trace stencils, make lines, simple designs, shapes and letters.

Toddlers can stab holes in the clay with an old pencil or tongue depressor, stick toothpicks or match sticks into the clay or gouge it with an old table knife.

When the clay gets choppy, have the child help you push it back into semi-smooth condition—this is a good hand exercise too; or warm it up again in your oven.

Comments: To develop muscle strength, you must overload the muscles slightly. Children will happily overload their hand and arm muscles in an activity that's fun, like this one. When they get bored with it, as they will, cover the tray with plastic and put it out of sight for a few weeks.

It helps to warm the tray slightly on a radiator before using it.

74. / The Elastic Eight

For:

Improving the grip on chalk or pencil.
Loosening, strengthening and coordinating the muscles of fingers, hand, wrist, arm and shoulder that are used in printing and handwriting.
Crossing the midline of the body (related to balance and flexibility).

Age: Primary grades. May be used profitably by younger children if they are given fairly close supervision, feedback and help.

The Elastic Eight

Materials: Chalk and chalkboard; a chair to stand on at the chalkboard.

Directions: The child stands before the chalkboard preferably on a chair. This is to reinforce proper body balance, and this position also adds interest and novelty to the activity. The teacher places a small eight (∞) on its side, on the chalkboard at about the child's chin height, and says, "Pretend the eight is made out of elastic. We're going to stretch it a little wider each time you go over the eight with your chalk." With each tracing of the lying-down eight, the design grows a bit wider until the child is reaching far to the right and across his body far to the left. We remind him frequently to keep the motions fluid, as though his fingers are skating across ice.

Comments: There are quite a few children whose body movements, fine motor movements, and often ocular movements are restricted and rigid, when moving across their own central axis (center of gravity). These children often have uncertain body balance, and are uncomfortable when trying to do any task that requires use of the right hand on the left side of the body (or vice versa). This is known as the midline problem and such a problem may subtly interfere with handwriting, reading or learning in general. The Elastic Eight game, in the most gentle and yet persuasive way, helps children become used to crossing the body's midline.

75. / Don't Spill The Coke

For:

> Midline problems. (Some children avoid reaching across their centers of gravity to their left sides with the right hand: see previous game's comments.)

Coordinating and strengthening the shoulder, arm, and hand muscles that are used together in printing and writing.

Age: Primary ages. Children will require adult supervision and feedback in order to gain the maximum benefits.

Materials: Chalkboard and chalk. A chair to stand on at the chalkboard (or footprints or chalk marks to stand *on* to hold the lower body fixed); a ball point pen.

Directions: With a ball point pen, the teacher should draw a drinking glass on the child's thumb, and a straw sticking straight up from it (see illustration). Children with problems in handwriting often lift their elbows and tip their hands, arms or body when writing at the board to avoid crossing their midlines. Next you say, "Let's draw concentric diamonds (or circles) but as you draw, don't let your hand tip—*don't tip the coke*. Keep the glass and straw upright no matter where the chalk line needs to go."

To start, the teacher places four chalk dots on the chalkboard which, when connected, will form a diamond. As the child completes the diamond, drawing lines dot to dot, the teacher places four more dots on the chalkboard. The new dots, when connected by the child, will form a slightly larger diamond surrounding the first diamond. The teacher keeps adding sets of four dots, and the child keeps forming larger and larger diamonds. Eventually, the child *may* be able to provide his or her own dots. (Keep in mind that the average age for *copying* a diamond is six and one-half.)

Variations: Children can use the "coke and straw" position for other chalkboard drawings, printing or writing.

Don't Spill The Coke

This exercise is largely a corrective one for problem printers and handwriters and should be done individually or in very small groups to give the child much guidance and feedback.

Comments: This activity exercises and coordinates the team of muscles in the upper body which must work together in rather precise ways in writing.

Keep in mind that children need both (a) free and unstructured chalkboard exercise where *no* attempt is made to isolate and control specific muscles, *and* (b) exercises like this one for isolating and strengthening specific muscles.

Although it is a fairly high level exercise, even uncoordinated children get caught up in the activity and concentrate happily for relatively long periods of practice.

76. / Writing With Rope

For:

Emphasizing the tactile and kinesthetic components of the writing process.
Getting the feel of a continuous, smooth line as used in cursive writing.
Helping to alleviate inappropriate back-tracking, reversing or lifting the pencil.

Writing With Rope

Age: Primarily for children who are beginning cursive writing, or who are having difficulties with cursive writing. (Of course, it is possible and desirable to use shorter strings to print with, or to draw shapes and simple designs. See Rope Shapes I, p. 182.)

Materials: A ball of light flexible rope or heavy cord, long enough to write a name with.

Directions: After the child has practiced writing his name in increasingly larger dimensions on the chalkboard and/or on paper, he may obtain a different perspective and additional feedback information (tactile and kinesthetic) by writing his name on the floor, in giant dimensions, using flexible rope or cord. He may write his name on a large sheet of (shelf) paper, put it on the floor and then go over it with rope; he may lightly sketch his name in chalk on a carpet and then lay down the rope over it; or he may work directly onto the unmarked floor with the rope. If the teacher (or an older child) can take the time to accompany him on his rope journey and offer help as needed, the child will be able to see and correct any errors in the formation of letters as they occur.

Variations: Children also benefit from drawing numbers, letters or simple shapes with any available materials, such as sticks, pebbles or buttons, yarn, cardboard strips, even rows of juice cans or milk cartons. Each experience adds something to the child's perceptual organization abilities.

20.

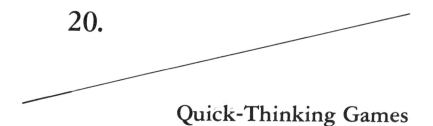

Quick-Thinking Games

A mind that can react quickly and work at various paces, perhaps under some stress or with conflicting background sound or movements, has a considerable advantage in a learning situation. The skill of automatic, quick mental reaction can be improved with practice. An uproarious game, where everyone both succeeds and fails, is one good place for children to begin to learn this skill.

77. / On And Off the Blanket

The game develops:

> Quick reaction to verbal signals. (The child integrates hearing, thinking and doing.)
> Coordination, balance and agility.

Age: All ages.

Materials: An old blanket or bedspread. In the absence of a blanket, a chalk line can be used for a front-and-back-of-the-line variation.

Directions: Children stand around the blanket and follow the leader's instructions: children jump *only* when the word "everyone" is used.

> "Everyone jump *on* the blanket!" (Everyone jumps just to inside edge of blanket.)

On And Off The Blanket

"Everyone jump *off* the blanket." (Everyone jumps just outside the blanket.) Now—to confuse the issue, say,

"Jump on the blanket." (Some will jump, and they lose a turn.)

Mix above commands in various ways, fast or slow, loud or soft, for a bang-up fun game.

Variation: Use "Simon Says" for a signal if this is easier.

Comments: A good socializing or reward game. Even small children who don't understand humor very well get the joke here. Encourage humor; discourage silliness. Tell children that balance is an important part of the game; sprawling or overjumping earns a "strike." Three strikes and you must lose a turn.

78. / Point To Knees And Count To Three

For:

> Body awareness.
> Quick reaction to verbal and visual signals.
> Social skills: taking turns, picking a friend, etc.
> Connecting body parts language to the touching of body parts (auditory-tacticle-visual match).

Age: All ages.

Materials: None.

Point To Knees And Count To Three

Directions: Children sit in a circle. Child #1 stands in the center with one hand partly over her eyes so she can peek through and the other hand extended, pointing. (The teacher may be the first "It" to demonstrate.) Child #1 turns slowly and suddenly stops, pointing to any child who has not had a turn and says, "Point to knees, one—two—three!" The child to whom "It" points must touch his knees before "It" gets to "three."

Variation: If children are young, or just beginning to learn the game, you could have "It" count to five, seven or even ten.

Comments: Children learn by watching others perform, as well as by performing themselves. If "It" cannot think up a body part, the teacher can whisper one in her ear. It might be a good idea, especially with very young children, to discuss and/or touch various body parts before beginning the game.

79. / Hot Potato Ball

For:

>   Making quick visual and motor movements involving space, speed and direction.
>   Social skills: accepting own and partner's goofs; perhaps losing a turn.
>   Concepts of size, texture and weight.

Age: All ages.

Materials: A collection of balls of varying sizes and materials, including any or all of the following: a large beach ball, a basketball, a soccer-sized ball, a Nerf ball, a yarn ball, large and small wiffle balls, a softball, a hand ball, a tennis ball, any rubber balls, a golf ball, a jacks ball, a marble, a bean bag or two.

Directions:

Version 1 (especially appropriate for young children). Place a variety of balls in a large box. Have children sit in a circle or better, in two rows across from one another so they can roll the balls straight back and forth to each other. The teacher takes a ball from the box and rolls it to Child #1, who rolls it to Child #2, and so on down the line. Waiting until the ball is part way or all the way down the line, the teacher starts another ball, preferably of a contrasting size or texture. Children may take a second to feel the ball, but should move it on to the next child rather quickly. Most children are highly intrigued by the contrast in weight, texture and size of the assortment of balls.

Version 2. "Illustrate" a story by passing or tossing various sized balls and bean bags. Just any traditional or original story, possibly involving some type of chase, will do fine. For example, tell the story of Peter Rabbit (with modifications). "Once upon a time there was a cute little navy blue rabbit named Peter" (pass around the navy blue bean bag, and with every reference to a motion by Peter Rabbit, pass it around again.) His mother (pass around the playground ball) warned him never to go near the garden. But Peter (bean bag) forgot and went directly into the garden and began to nibble the lettuce. The farmer's son (pass the

Hot Potato Ball

basketball) saw Peter, but thought he was cute and didn't disturb him. The farmer (pass the beachball) saw Peter (bean bag) and began to chase him with his gun. Peter ran under the fence and into the woods (pass bean bag quickly.) The farmer chased him (pass beachball quickly), and the farmer's son ran after the farmer (pass basketball quickly) shouting, 'Don't shoot that nice little rabbit.'" (Make up your own ending.) Stories could involve car chases, wild animals, giants, space-people, airplanes, Indians, you name it. Children may make up a story by taking turns adding on a sentence at a time.

Version 3. "Fox and Squirrel." Children sit in a circle. A bean bag is the squirrel and a ball is the fox. The "squirrel" is passed or tossed around the circle and the "fox" is also started around the circle. We can help the fox by passing the ball quickly. We can help the squirrel two ways: by passing quickly and by reversing direction. The fox may reverse direction too, but only *after* the squirrel does so. Optional: if the fox catches up with the squirrel, whoever is holding both gets a strike against him or her. Three strikes and you must lose a turn.

Version 4. Several balls and/or bean bags may be passed in a single direction. The object is to not get caught holding more than one bean bag or ball at a time.

See also Ten Trips, p. 206.

80. / Hit-And-Run Dodge Ball

For:

Many quick mental and physical changes requiring spatial judgment. Balance, coordination, agility, endurance and eye-hand coordination. Social skills: following simple rules, getting caught, etc.

Age: Primary grades. Younger children can play some versions.

Materials: A baseball bat (plastic or wooden), a wiffle ball (if indoors); a softball or a playground ball for some versions. A baseball tee is helpful for children who may not be able to hit a pitched ball, and a few obstacles are good but not mandatory: a ladder, a balance beam, hoops, a mat or two. The game requires a large space.

Directions: The game may be played with as few as two people, or a small group of children. It is an ideal game for an adult and child to play while doing remedial perceptual-motor work. Many skills are involved, and precisely the ones the child needs may be worked in.

Arrange a home plate (with a baseball tee, if desired) and a series of about three obstacles leading to first base. There should be ten feet or so of space between the obstacles and twenty feet of space between home plate and the beginning of the

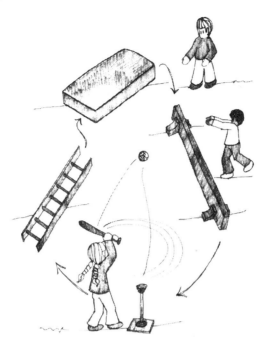

Hit-And-Run Dodge Ball

obstacles. Obstacles might include a ladder to run through, a mat to do a somersault on, and a couple of hoops to jump into; or instead of obstacles, special areas for fancy jumps may be arranged.

The idea is for Child #1 to bat (or kick) a ball (from a tee, or pitched, or rolled) and run through the obstacle course while a teammate, Child #2, retrieves the ball. Child #1 is safe while in contact with any bases and *while on the obstacles*. Between the obstacles, any fielders who have the ball (Child #2), may throw or roll it at Child #1's feet. If fielders hit the runner, runner does not get a point; if he or she gets home safe, Child #1 scores a point. In either case, the turn should pass to the next child. Fielders may not get closer than ten (or so) feet to the runner when throwing the ball. The runner may not wait in a safe zone more than five seconds after completing the obstacle.

Variations: The game may readily be made easier or harder by adding more or fewer, easy or difficult, obstacles; by using larger or smaller balls; and by rolling or pitching the ball to the batter instead of using a baseball tee.

Instead of a baseball bat, a golf club, stick, or no bat at all could be used. Child #1 may throw or kick the ball.

Comments: Strong motivation and fast movements are built into this game. Therefore, it is very good practice for the lethargic, heavy-footed child.

21.

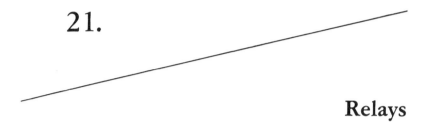

Relays

When you get right down to it, why do teachers still persist in having their children play relay games? There are a number of very good reasons. Starting with what I feel are the most important, some of these are the following:

1. The element of team competition is not personally threatening, yet it lends an air of excitement and delight to the game.
2. Rather routine skills which may have become boring, but which still need practice, (such as hopping, jumping, balancing a bean bag) take on new meaning in a team relay.
3. Children will extend themselves in a relay and will use a given skill less self-consciously, more rapidly, more rhythmically, and more automatically when involved in a low-key race.
4. The mechanical setup of a relay (taking turns, moving up a line) is itself a skill useful in many sports and games and teaches cooperative play.
5. The teacher can arrange many small teams so there is little waiting for a turn.
6. The teacher can match children weak in motor skills (for example, all these would be in the #1 position of their various teams). He also can avoid putting self-conscious children last, when excitement reaches a peak.

81. / Jumping Relay

The game develops:

> Balance, agility, leg strength and overall body strength.
> Rhythmic coordination of the body.
> Quick changes.
> Social skills, team work, winning and losing.
> Concepts and vocabulary of body parts, positions, space, distance, speeds,
> direction, right-left, etc.

Age: All ages. Types of jumps must be selected according to ability of children. Young children may practice all jumps without the relay aspect.

Materials: None. Two rope or chalk lines are helpful to mark the starting-finishing line and the turning line. A set of cards or sheets showing sketches of various jumps often are helpful, especially in explaining the game for the first time. (Don't worry if your sketches are crude.)

Directions: One advantage of this relay is that less adept children may do easy jumps; more adept children may do difficult jumps. This game is particularly appropriate for a class where there is a wide range of motor ability. Arrange starting line and turning line any distance apart (perhaps only ten feet for young children); discuss, show pictures, demonstrate and have children practice the various jumps that will be used in the game (three to six types).

Types of jumps to include:

Forward	Scissor jumps (apart-together)
Backward	Straddle jumps (apart)
Sideways	Zig-zag (feet together, jump diagonally left,
(left foot leading)	then diagonally right)
(right foot leading)	Any of above with arms crossed, outstretched, etc.

Divide class into teams of about four children each. It is better to avoid "choosing up" sides. Children could form teams by lot, but it is preferable to have the teacher assign children to each team, in order to balance them skill-wise. Thus each team can have the same number of less adept, more adept and average children. Discuss winning: that it is not important, but makes the game a little more interesting and that everyone who plays the game wins in the sense of getting stronger legs, etc.

Jumping Relay

Now, the first person on each team does the forward jump to the rope line; he turns and jumps back to his team and touches the hand of Child #2 as he crosses the finish line and goes to rear of line. The second child does a sideways jump up and back; Child #3 does a straddle jump and Child #4 does the zig-zag jump. Remember, Child #2 may not start until Child #1 has crossed the finish line and touched #2's hand. When all children on one team have returned to original positions, the game is over. However, let late-starters continue until all children have had a turn.

Variations:
1. Walking steps may be used: forward, backward, sideways; toes pointed in, toes out, tiptoe; eyes closed, eyes on target; sideways, crossing one foot over, or step-close; forward criss-cross, backward criss-cross.
2. Animal walks may be used as bear, crab, snake, lame dog.
3. Various locomotor patterns: skipping, hopping, galloping, running, walking, crawling.
4. A combination of jumps, walks, animal walks and locomotor patterns:
   first child on each team walks backward,
   second child on each team walks crab style,
   third child on each team skips,
   fourth child on each team zig-zag jumps.
5. All children may do the same jump or walk, etc.

Comments: Sometimes the practice session may be more instructive than the actual game. You may say, "When you become pretty good at practicing these jumps, we'll have a relay race." Sort of sneaky, but children will immediately set out to work hard to convince you they *are* pretty good and ready for the "real game."

82. / Through The Tunnel And/Or Over The Bridge

For:

> Attention span extension. (Child must watch for the ball which is often out of sight.)
> Quick reactions.
> Object handling skills: visual tracking; eye-hand and eye-body coordination.
> Social skills: working with a small team.

Age: Primary age.

Materials: A playground ball or other large ball for each team. A balloon or bean bag may be used.

Directions: Children should understand the relay technique of moving up or down a line before playing this game. Children who have never played relay races should practice in a more simple relay such as bead-in-a-spoon carry. (See p. 158.)

In this game, passing an object backward *down* a line is used.

1. The ball is started at the front of the line and passed backward;

Through The Tunnel And/Or Over The Bridge

2. Last person in the line carries object to front of line, and

3. Starts passing the ball backward again.

4. When first child is back in original position, the relay ends.

To play "Over the Bridge," the ball is passed over the head, backward.

To play "Through the Tunnel," the ball is passed football style through the legs.

To play "Through the Tunnel and Over the Bridge," the ball is passed alternately through the legs and over head (backward).

Games with a slight (repeat, *slight*) element of competition can be hilarious, good fun, and stimulating for children to try harder. There probably should never be more than one competitive game in any one day's perceptual motor game time.

Comments: Although the competitive element of the relay is useful, it is important that it be kept within bounds (i.e., played down). Usually the teacher should discuss before the game starts that winning adds a little fun to the game but is of no real value in itself. Fun *is* important, but winning is *not*. (Yes, Virginia, it *is* really true that it doesn't matter whether you win or lose, it's how you play the game.)

I harp on the fact that everyone who plays the game wins because "you are teaching your body some new skills, etc."

Very little need be said about or to the winners. The entire class should be congratulated often: "You are all good players and such good sports. Let's clap for all of us."

83. / Bead-In-A-Spoon Carry

For:

Eye-hand-body coordination and balance.

Combining carefulness and speed.

Relay game skills: taking turns, passing the spoon to a partner, paying attention to one's job in spite of distractions.

Age: Primary grades. Younger children may play a modified or non-relay version of the game.

Materials: A spoon and a wooden bead for each team; extra spoons and beads for pre-game practice (preferably one of each for each child).

Directions: Divide the class into several teams of about three or four children each. Teams line up behind leaders, who stand on a starting line. (Many small teams are better than a few long lines.) The first child on each team (the leader) holds a spoon with a round wooden bead in it. On the signal "go" each leader moves as quickly as possible to a turning line about fifteen feet away (further if

Bead-In-A-Spoon Carry

desired), touches the line with a foot, turns and comes back to the starting place. He or she passes the spoon and bead to the next child in line who repeats the operation. The first team to complete all trips wins a point. If a child drops the bead, she must retrieve it, replace it in her spoon and continue to walk from the place where she stopped.

Comments: Younger children might carry square wooden beads. Occasionally a very shaky child may need to have a special object to carry in place of a bead, for example, a small magnet that will stick to the spoon. Is this fair to the other children? Yes, most other children can readily accept that sometimes one child needs special treatment. Especially if winning, point collecting and competition are used with a *very* light touch in all school activities.

84. / Toss-Jump-Pick

For:

> Coordinating eyes, hands, body and feet.
> Space judging.

Age: Primary grades. Younger children will enjoy practicing the game as a non-relay activity.

Materials: A bean bag for each child or team.

Directions: The teacher should demonstrate, and children should practice separately before using the activity as a relay.

Toss-Jump-Pick

With children standing on the starting line,

> "Toss the bean bag in front of you onto the floor, any distance that you can jump over. Next, jump over the bean bag so that all parts of the foot are ahead of the bag. If you didn't quite jump over it, the bean bag must be picked up and you return to your original throwing place for another try."

> "Assume you did jump over the bean bag. Now you turn your body and without moving your feet, bend over, pick up the bean bag and toss it ahead of you again. Repeat the toss, the jump and the pick up until you get to the turn-around line, and come back to the starting line the same way."

For the relay, divide the class into many small teams, so there will be more participation and less waiting. At the signal "go," the first child on each team tosses-jumps-picks the bean bag to the turn-around line, returns the same way and gives the bean bag to the next team members. The first team to finish wins.

Comments: Most children need considerable practice to judge what distance to throw the bean bag so that they can jump over it.

22.

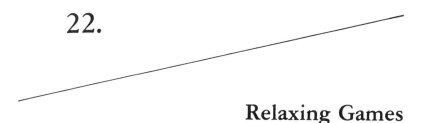

Relaxing Games

Very few children (and for that matter, all too few adults) are aware of mounting tension or overstimulation within themselves and still fewer know how to calm down deliberately and relax at the appropriate time.

Relaxation games should be taught often to show children how they can be in charge of their various gears and speeds.

For the teacher's sanity too, a relaxation game after vigorous activity unifies the class and prepares the children for table or desk work to follow. Relaxation games are often used at the end of perceptual-motor time but may be used anytime children become overstimulated.

85. / The Magic Feather

The game develops:

> Body awareness: visual-auditory-tactile.
> Relaxation: holding the body immobile without tension.

Age: Primary ages, kindergarten. Younger children can play the game, with more relaxed expectations.

The Magic Feather

Materials: A long, preferably stiff feather is desirable but not necessary. A fold of cloth (scarf or handkerchief), a loop of yarn, or even the eraser end of a pencil will do.

Directions: Children sit in a circle. Child #1 closes his or her eyes and then the magic feather (in the hand of the teacher or Child #2) will descend and touch Child #1 softly on the face, neck, hands, arms or hair. The child, without opening her eyes, is to touch that exact spot on herself with the *tip* of the index finger. Children of age four or older who consistently miss the spot by more than 3/8" may have body awareness problems and should receive extra practice in this area.

The turn passes until as many children as possible have had a chance to point to the spot where the magic feather touched.

Due to more nerve endings, face and hands are easier to spot than other parts of the body. Children may be touched on shoulders, back, legs, etc., through their clothing too. For this, the quill end of the feather may be used.

Children learn from watching as well as doing; children may take turns working the feather.

Comments: This game is almost magical in its ability to capture and hold children's interest. They love to be touched in this way and to have the undivided attention of the class for a short time in a non-threatening way. At the beginning of the game it should be explained that if the child is within 3/8" (hold up your fingers to show), that is a good response.

If a child misses more than this I may say, "You were this close," holding up thumb and forefinger. The child *should* receive some tactful feedback from the teacher as to how close she is able to come to the touched spot.

The game is a good way of informally spotting body awareness or tactile difficulties. Keep in mind that most children can touch the end of the nose with a finger tip, eyes closed, by age four.

86. / Stone School

For:

Relaxation, some right and left awareness.

Social skills: taking turns, accepting good luck or bad luck and accepting minor frustration and gentle competition.

The joy of a simple game with a few effortless rules.

Age: All ages.

Materials: A small pebble or other object that can be hidden in the hand.

Directions: Children sit in a row on the floor, marked by a chalk line if desired; this is "nursery school." Behind each child is a chair, "kindergarten." The teacher (or any leader) hides her hands behind her back and then holds fists (both closed) out before Child #1, who guesses which hand the pebble is in. If the child guesses incorrectly, he stays seated on the floor. If he guesses correctly, he moves to kindergarten (sits on the chair). The turn passes to Child #2, #3, etc. Optional: the teacher continues giving turns to all remaining "floor" children until all are in "kindergarten." After the children move through "kindergarten" (seated on chair) they go to "first grade" (standing on chair).

It is important that turns continue until *all* children have reached first grade and are standing on their chairs. The game also may be played on stairs, indoors or out.

Theoretically, the first child to reach first grade is the winner, but I find it's best to say rather little or nothing about winning. If the children bring it up, I may say (as usual) that everyone wins in the game because you're learning new skills (how to follow simple rules).

Variations: The teacher may emphasize left and right hands as the game is played.

Comments: There are several suggestions that help to make this a game children absolutely adore: the teacher should experiment and find what works best with his or her class; the teacher's attitude and approach to the game is more important than the game itself; and the teacher should discuss that (1) this is a game of chance, and skill has little or nothing to do with it; (2) you may be lucky or unlucky; (3) if you're lucky, you get to move "up through the grades of school" quickly; and (4) if you're unlucky, you get more turns, so either way it's fun.

Stone School

Comments on sportsmanship: Sportsmanship is a hard skill for children to learn, and for most children it takes patient practice over many years. When children seem to be having a rash of bad sportsmanship, we may take one or several of these options:

1. Avoid any competitive games for a while.
2. Discuss the "hard parts" of the game before starting (hard = frustrating).
3. Discuss and hopefully role-play what you might do or say when you win, when you lose. Children should be taught, in concrete, operational terms, how to accept their own and their friends' goofs.
4. Avoid over-praising winners; the winner may be recognized with a smile or comment such as "John's in first grade now."
5. Single out children who show good sportsmanship and mention this briefly: "I like the way Brad and Patty say 'Good try' to their classmates."
6. Praise the whole group for effort and consideration. We clap a lot for ourselves.

87. / Clock Watching

For:

Bringing relaxation under conscious control.

Time, space and number relationships.

Body awareness: alternately tensing and relaxing whole body or differentiating parts of body.

Holding the body immobile for gradually extended periods of time.

Attention and concentration.

Age: All ages. Older children will be able to perform a more refined control of the body for longer periods of time and with a more advanced degree of awareness of the internal and external processes. Older children may understand more fully the concept of seconds of time.

Materials: Any clock with a sweep second hand that is easily visible. For some variations a small light feather or a stop watch is helpful.

Introductory comments: All the variations of this game are based on children's "inherent" fascination with the second hand of a clock. It is important to remember that young children can play the game without fully understanding the concept of seconds of time. For them we may say "Freeze until the red (second) hand gets to the three," or "Freeze until the red (second) hand gets to here" or "Freeze until the red (second) hand passes five dots." The teacher should count aloud, and clearly signal when to start and stop.

Primary age children enjoy knowing that they have a "built-in stop watch," i.e., it takes approximately one second to say "one chimpanzee" or "one thousand and one."

Directions:

Version 1. "Freeze the body." "Hold your body in any *comfortable* position while the red second hand moves five dots. I'll count with it. Try not to move any part of your body, except maybe your eyes. Ready, Freeze! One-two-three-four-five. Relax. Good holding."

Version 2. "Tighten the body." Explain and practice tightening the entire body and relaxing (or resting) the whole body. At the signal, "Tighten," children make their whole bodies as rigid as possible, and hold while the teacher counts to

Clock Watching

five "chimpanzees"; then, on signal, rest while the teacher counts again to five chimpanzees.

Version 3. "Statue Hold." Children may stand in hoops or rope circles. On signal, children may do a given exercise, jumping jacks, bends, wiggles or shakes. At the sound of a whistle or tom-tom, they are to freeze "in mid-air" and hold while the teacher counts with the clock about four or five seconds. Relax. Change to another type of movement; repeat. Children will enjoy changing circles, too.

Version 4. "Tighten and relax, right and left." Mark the right wrist with a rubber band. Practice tightening and relaxing a single arm or leg, without counting. When children can tighten *only* a single part of the body while keeping the remainder of the body relaxed, they are ready to add the counts. "Hold up your right arm. Get ready to tighten it very, very stiffly. Ready, tighten! One-two-three-four-five. Relax."

"Now, let's try both arms. Remember, your legs, head and body should be taking a little rest. Only the arms are working. Ready, tighten! One-two-three-four-five. Relax. Good tightening."

Variations: (a) Tighten the arm *gradually*, first a little, then tighter and tighter until full tension is reached on the count of five. Relax gradually with a count. (b) Tighten right arm and right leg only. Tighten right arm and left leg only, etc.

Version 5. "Feather Drift." Drop a very small light feather from a height. Hopefully it will take two or more seconds to reach the floor. "Pretend we are tiny light feathers, falling from a bird's wing high up in a tree. See if you can take a full five seconds to drift to the floor. By the count of three, you should only be about halfway down. Ready, drift down slowly, one-two-three, etc."

Version 6. "Estimate the seconds" (older children only). Children may sit on chairs. After explaining how a stop watch works, turn the watch face down in the teacher's hand. The child is to estimate when ten seconds have gone by and stand up. At the signal "start," Child #1 starts counting "one chimpanzee, etc." aloud or silently. When he thinks ten seconds have elapsed, he stands up and the teacher stops the watch. Turn the watch face up and see if the estimate was close to being correct. Vary the number of seconds. Children might work the watch for each other. Praise effort, not success and do not expect exactness.

88. / Localizing Sounds

For:

Alert relaxation of an entire group.
Space-distance direction concepts; pointing to the origin of a sound.

Localizing Sounds

Listening skills: identifying and labelling, remembering and reproducing sounds or sound patterns.

Age: All ages.

Materials: For the first version, none. For the second version, any noise-making or musical instrument (tom-tom, bell, drum, autoharp, whistle, metronome); or classroom or kitchen tool (egg-beater, spoons, chalk and chalkboard, wooden blocks, etc.).

Directions:

Version 1. Child #1 sits on a chair in the center of the room wearing a blindfold. Child #2 tiptoes anywhere in the room, preferably a far corner, and says, "Hello." Child #1 points to the place from which the "hello" came; the point should be fairly exact. If it is in error, the teacher may say "You're close. Listen again," and signal Child #2 to say "Hello" again. If Child #1 still cannot point accurately, the teacher may move Child #1's hand to the correct angle. Optional: the teacher may then ask, "Do you know who spoke the 'Hello?'" and offer hints if they are needed, for example, "It was a tall boy with brown hair and blue eyes, and he's wearing a football shirt today."

Version 2. (a) Child #1 sits blindfolded in a chair. Child #2 takes any noise- or music-making implement to another part of the room and makes a noise (or patterned rhythm with it, for example, she taps three times with a drum). Child #1 first points to the place the sounds came from and then (optional) identifies the instrument or implement, and finally (also optional) repeats the pattern (three taps) by clapping three times.

(b) Child #1 is blindfolded. Child #2 takes a common household or classroom object to a far place and makes the characteristic noise with it. The object may be very easy to identify for young children (for example, a pair of scissors cutting paper) or may be more difficult (for example, the sound of a pencil marking on paper, or chalk marking on a chalkboard).

Comments: To prevent Child #1's identifying the location from Child #2's footsteps, it is fun to have the rest of the children make cover-up scraping noises with their shoes until Child #2 arrives at his location. (See also "Who is Knocking at my Door," p. 25.)

23.

Rhythmics

One of the major goals of perceptual motor games is *automatic* control of the body. This is to free the brain from constant monitoring of body motions in order to concentrate on other things (such as subject matter).

Another goal is the smooth, flowing change of body direction, speed or force which becomes so effortless and efficient that confidence, pleasure, play, and physical or mental work become intertwined.

Rhythmic games are a pleasant way of coordinating (1) brain (or mental) sequencing of body commands with (2) appropriate body responses to the point where muscles react with minimal brain messages.

Rhythmic activities need not and should not be only musical. Any repetitive motion, such as see-sawing, skipping or bouncing a ball, is a rhythmic activity.

As the child moves into academic learning, a rhythmic sense will benefit speech, reading and writing.

89. / This Old Man

The game develops:

> Rhythm awareness: clapping rhythmic beat.
> Combining gestures with verbal signals (auditory-visual-motor match).
> Using simple musical instruments.

Age: All ages; however, children should not be expected to keep really good rhythm until about age six, or even later.

This Old Man

Materials: None. Some simple musical instruments such as wood blocks, or tom-toms may be used if desired.

Directions: Children may perform any (or a combination) of the following, while singing: (1) act out the numbers by holding up fingers; (2) act out the objects mentioned in the song; (3) clap rhythm; or (4) use simple instruments, such as ordinary wood blocks.

Verse: This old man, he played one, he played knick-knack on my thumb,
With a knick-knack, paddy-wack, give a dog a bone,
This old man came rolling home.
This old man, he played two, he played knick-knack on my shoe,

Etc.	three	knee
	four	door
	five	hive
	six	sticks
	seven	oven (or heaven)
	eight	gate
	nine	line (or tine)
	ten	hen.

This is another old favorite song with a very strong beat. Its many short verses provide for a variety of rhythmic activities and allow every child to have a turn with an instrument. Children need not do all verses; but if they do, they will have received extensive rhythmic practice.

Comments: In any group, there are generally wide differences in the ability to clap rhythm. Some children have a natural feel for it; others have great difficulties. I have noticed many of those with poor rhythmic sense can do quite well during short periods of high motivation.

Here is what may be done to motivate: let those with a good beat start taking turns leading (sitting in front of) the group (one, two or three children for each verse), and/or take turns with one or more musical instruments. As the less adept children watch, they often seem to catch the mood. Eventually every child should get a turn with an instrument and/or leading.

In my experience, it is better to have only one or two (or so) musical instruments in use at one time. Many instruments may be distracting, but this is a matter for the teacher to experiment with.

90. / Teddy Bear

A jump-rope chant adapted for children who can't yet jump rope.

For:

Whole body rhythmic coordination.

Matching gestures and body actions to verbal signals (auditory-visual-kinesthetic match).

Balance.

Game skills: following a circle path with proper space between each child.

Age: First-graders, kindergartners and pre-schoolers.

Materials: A tom-tom with which the teacher thumps the beat is helpful. A rope circle on the floor is helpful to mark the path.

Directions: Children may practice clapping only, then gestures only, while seated. They may practice marching only, while walking around a large circle. Eventually children may march, perform gestures, clap and chant simultaneously.

Verse 1: Teddy Bear, Teddy Bear turn around (children turn)
           "   "   touch the ground (children touch floor)
           "   "   shine your shoes (children flick shoe)
           "   "   skidoo (children jump up and down).

Teddy Bear

Verse 2: Teddy Bear, Teddy Bear go upstairs (step high)
          "   "   say your prayers (fold hands)
          "   "   turn out the light (reach up; pull hand down)
          "   "   Now, goodnight (fold hands beside cheek).

Variations: This is a good chant to accompany trampoline jumping, or you might want to do this chant while parading in a long line around the room or playground.

91. / Don't Say "Ain't"

For:

Clapping rhythm.
Coordinating verbal and motor performance.

Age: Easy enough for very young children; older children enjoy some difficult variations.

Materials: None.

Directions: Although beating the rhythm of a song is often quite difficult, some songs or chants, as this one, are so compelling in their rhythm, that even a child with poor rhythm can do well.

Children sit in a circle and clap while saying the following rhyme:

    Don't say "ain't"; your mother will faint!
  (clap)   (clap)   (clap)   (clap)

Don't Say "Ain't"

Your father will fall in a bucket of paint!
   (clap)   (clap)   (clap)   (clap)

Your sister will cry, your brother will die;
   (clap)   (clap)   (clap)   (clap)

The cat and the dog will say "Goodbye!"
   (clap)   (clap)   (clap)   (clap)

Variations:

1. On the first beat, clap. On the second beat, tap the foot. Continue throughout the chant.
2. Alternate a clap and a snap of the fingers.
3. Instead of two motions alternating, use all four motions, for example:

DON'T   SAY   AIN'T   YOUR   MOTHER   WILL   FAINT (pause).
snap left; snap right; tap left; tap right; snap left; snap right; tap left; tap right

Comments: So easy and compelling is the rhythm, that every child will succeed at some version.

92. / Clap With The Metronome

For:

Integration of motor (kinesthetic), visual and auditory rhythm.
Time concepts and time measurements, including relationships between time, distance and speed.

Age: All ages, especially primary. The metronome provides a valuable learning experience whether or not children are able to articulate or fully understand the time concepts involved. Permit children to take from the experience what they can.

Materials: A metronome (bought, begged or borrowed); some parts of the game may be adapted to another rhythm instrument, such as a tom-tom, if no metronome is available.

Introductory comments: All children are spellbound by the metronome, as well they should be. In introducing one to a class, the teacher should explain that it is very delicate or fragile (explaining these words), and is something like a watch, in that it ticks and may be set to measure seconds and other units of time. The teacher then may demonstrate the various speeds of the metronome, explain-

Clap With The Metronome

ing that as the weight is raised, the metronome clicks more slowly, and as the numbers go down there are fewer beats per minute. As the weight is slid lower, the numbers increase; so do the beats per minute, and the clicks get faster.

After such an explanation, children may be allowed, in turn, to adjust the weight carefully and regulate the clicks. Only the teacher should hold the metronome at this time to prevent it from dropping.

During the game and when the game is over, the metronome should be kept out of reach, for example on a high shelf.

Primary and pre-school children, of course, cannot understand the complex relationship between the height of weight, the width of the swing of the arm, the numbers on the metronome face, the speed of the clicks, and the relationship of all these to a clock. However, children *will* have a valuable experience with faster and slower, up and down, and back and forth. And some day, the dimly remembered click-click-click of the metronome will fit in with the tick-tick-tick of a grandfather clock and the sweep of an electric clock's second hand.

Children may take turns (individually or a few at a time, while learning) clapping, tapping, marching or jumping to the beat of the metronome. As with all rhythmic activities, some will have more success than others. Children may clap while watching the metronome's arm swing, then try clapping with the metronome out of sight.

Some children may be quite unable to match their claps to the metronome's slowest rhythm, but may do quite well with a bit faster rhythm. Even if a child *never* is able to match the metronome's beat, it is important that she enjoy the abundant experiential information that a metronome brings her.

24.

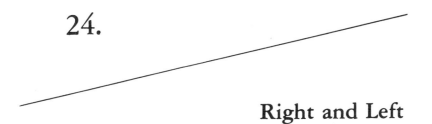

Right and Left

The idea of two sides of the body (laterality) emerges slowly but (hopefully) surely as the child grows in body awareness. The *naming* of right and left with words follows much later; the average age for this correct naming is six years old.

By the age of two we can begin to call a child's attention to the fact that he has one side which we adults call left and a side we call right. We may not use these exact words; we may say "your side that's near the door," or "the window side," or "the hand that's got the rubber band on," etc.

By the time the child is three, we should play many games where we mark one hand or foot (preferably always on the right side to avoid confusion), then have the child manipulate the marked and the unmarked hand or foot, as in the singing game, "Looby Loo."

93. / Wrist Weights

The game develops:

Right and left feel; right and left identification by name.
Weight concepts.

Age: All ages.

Materials: Any small weight that can be tied with tape around a child's wrist (and/or ankle). These can be purchased through athletic supply catalogues, made

Wrist Weights

or improvised. Ideally, the weight should be between eight and sixteen ounces. A parent made a set of wrist weights for our school by folding lead foil into a strip, sewing the strip inside brown leatherette, and attaching nylon Velcro strips for fasteners.

Directions: Children fasten the weight onto the right wrist (even if left-handed). We leave the weight on for at least fifteen minutes while we do other games or activities, such as a right-left singing game (Looby-Loo or Hokey-Pokey; see p. 178). We talk about left and right and match the right foot to the right hand, etc. After the weights are removed, we ask, "Which is your right hand?" They will remember. One-half hour later if we ask again, most will remember correctly. We are not disappointed if this knowledge cannot be articulated the next day. A non-verbal feeling is being developed, which will take months and years to mature.

Comments: A superb way of adding to a child's right-left information bank. In the wrist weight game, the difficult right-left concept is greatly facilitated by visual, tactile, verbal and most importantly, kinesthetic senses.

94. / Foot And Hand Prints

For:

>   Right and left awareness and naming.
>   Space judging.
>   Body awareness (matching feet and hands to variously spaced visual marks).

Age: All ages.

Materials: A set of fifteen or more pairs of cut-out poster board soles, preferably in two colors, as fifteen red rights and fifteen green lefts. A set of eight pairs of hand prints all in one color. Very easy to make: just draw around an adult shoe for footprint model, and around spread hand for handprint model. Foot and hand-prints also may be cut out of adhesive backed shelf liner or may be ordered from school equipment toy catalogues; markers for the right hand and/or foot if desired.

Directions: Discuss how our hands and soles match the curves of the cut-out model. Arrange footprints in an easily-walked pattern across the floor, all red prints for the right foot, green prints on the left. (Masking tape may be used to hold the prints down.) Explain that the right foot must step only on red and the left foot on green. Never mind if young children do not fully understand which is right and which is left. In *doing* this and other right-left games, they will become slowly, increasingly aware of their two sides. The teacher should give as much help as needed while children are moving through the course, perhaps having only one child go through at a time for a while. The teacher may want to mark the right toe with a rubber band, a ribbon around the ankle, or with an old large sock pulled over the shoe.

As the children become adept at the game, a few hand prints may be added to the right and left sides of the walking course. As the children spot a handprint, they should touch down a hand to match the handprint.

Variations: As children become still more skilled the teacher can vary the course in several ways:
1. Arrange footprints in curves, U-turns, closer together or far apart, etc.
2. Arrange a right-handed handprint on the left side of the walking course.
3. Arrange a *pair* of handprints (one right, one left) together here and there on the course.

Foot And Hand Prints

4. Let the footprints crawl over a chair, a board, or other obstacles.
5. Let the footprints point slightly in or out—child must twist a foot to match the footprint.

After you have done these variations, you or the children will no doubt have thought of still other footprint arrangements.

Comments: This is a no-fail game which all children and all ages love, at least for a while. Sometimes we call the game "Santa Claus's Footprints" if the prints are made of red and green cardboard. One could make bear or rhinoceros prints too, I suppose. Remember that children will require many hundreds of right-left experiences before they are able to name right and left accurately.

Prints could be made of felt too, which will cling to a carpet.

95. / Hokey-Pokey

For:

Right and left practice.
Rhythmic coordination of body.
Matching motor movements with words; reacting to verbal signals.

Age: Kindergarten and pre-school.

Materials: Rubber bands to mark the right wrist and/or ankle. A rope circle on the floor is helpful.

Directions: Although children should not be expected to be able to identify left and right on their bodies until age six, they need many opportunities to practice this difficult concept. This song and its cousin, "Looby Loo," are so charming and gay that children forget that they don't really quite understand left and right. Though many errors are inevitable, the game sweeps children along and helps them build onto whatever left-right understanding they may have. Rubber band markers (or magic marker dots)on the right hand or wrist are very helpful. The teacher should actively teach, help identify, discuss and otherwise emphasize the left and right point as much as possible, however, without causing any child to feel self-conscious about errors.

Comments: A rope on the floor in the form of a circle will help young children to understand "in" and "out" and will keep the game more orderly. To make the game easier, it is suggested that only the right one of the paired parts be used, i.e.,

Hokey-Pokey

the right hand, foot, ear, knee, shoulder, elbow, leg, arm, etc. Although the *teacher* probably will work hard during this game, it is important that the children feel relaxed and successful. Children will not be disturbed if the music stops from time to time while everyone gets his or her right foot in.

96. / Right And Left City

For:

> Higher level right and left discrimination (i.e., on another person).
> Eye-hand and whole body coordination.
> Planning one's action and verbalizing it before executing the action.

Age: Primary ages. The child should have essentially mastered the naming of right and left on himself before attempting to name right and left on a partner.

Materials: A light-weight hockey stick for each player (broomsticks might substitute for hockey sticks); a plastic puck for each pair of partners. The game should be played in a gym, lunchroom or outdoors. Most classrooms will not accommodate to the space required. A simpler version requiring a ball for each pair of children might be played in the classroom. Markers of 5 × 7 cards taped to the floor are a helpful visual support at first.

Directions: It is suggested that the game be played in small groups so that the teacher can be available to give feedback and correction of right and left errors.

Two children stand twenty to thirty feet apart. We are going to pretend that Child #1 is going to send a letter (the puck) across the room to Right City (the area on his partner's right), to Left City (the area on his partner's left) or Center City (directly in front of his partner). Now before Child #1 may send the puck across to his partner, he must "address the letter," that is, he must say to which city he is going to send the puck. The partner, Child #2, prepares to receive the puck. Then Child #2 takes his turn, stating where he will send *his* letter, and firing the hockey puck back to Child #1.

Right And Left City

Variation: Children may roll, kick, throw or bat a large ball to their partner's left or right.

Keeping score, if desired: While children are learning the game, it might be best *not* to keep score, as considerable concentration is required to execute the various steps. If and when it is deemed desirable to keep score, each successful block could count one point for the receiver, and each successful "letter" sent past the receiver would count one point for the sender. In practice, many young children appear to be relieved if they are not allowed to keep score.

Children should not choose "Center City" continuously.

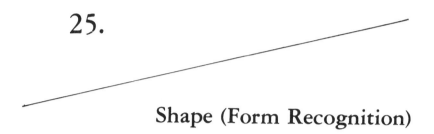

25.

Shape (Form Recognition)

If you visited several days in a nursery school or kindergarten, you surely would notice that a great to-do is made over the basic shapes: the circle, square, triangle, rectangle and diamond. It is absolutely essential that every child eventually be on very friendly terms with every curve, corner and line of these shapes or forms. When she knows the shapes upside-down and inside-out, she can begin to combine them in various ways, blending lines and curves, adding dots, tails, diagonals, corners. This is the beginning of printed letters, the eventual reading of which is a highly complex and difficult task.

97. / Rope Shapes I

The game develops:

> Form or shape recognition (visual perception); integration of visual, verbal, tactile and kinesthetic information.
> Object handling (drawing with rope).
> Cooperative play; following directions.
> Balance and locomotor skills.
> Vocabulary of space, direction, shape and size.

Age: All ages.

Materials: One six- or seven-foot rope for each child. (Very heavy twine would do in a pinch.) A tom-tom to indicate "Freeze and get ready for a change!"

Rope Shapes I

Directions: Give each child a rope and tell each to find a place on the floor where he can spread out his rope and make a circle, square or triangle, etc. (It would help to draw a circle, square, etc. on the chalkboard first.)

When the children have made their shapes, say, "Now we're going to walk around the outside of the shape, getting our feet as close to the rope as possible without quite touching it. Next, let's get inside the shape and jump in and out several times. Now step across the shape, walk it sideways, etc."

"Now look around you and see who else has made a shape like yours. Mary, you and Joe both made squares. Let's put your ropes together and make one big square. Everyone, combine your rope with another person's and make a larger shape. Let's walk around the inside of the new shape, jump over it, etc."

"Next let's put four ropes together and make a super-size circle, square, triangle, etc. (Hopefully not all the shapes will be alike.) Let's walk backward around this big shape, sideways, etc."

"Now let's leave the shapes as they are, but trade positions—move to your neighbor's shape and walk *it*, forward, backward, sideways. See if you can hop across it without disturbing the ropes. Trade again to another new shape, etc."

Comments: If you're buying new rope, any kind will do; however, sash cord can also be used for jumping rope. (See also Space Walk, p. 111.)

98. / Chalkboard Treasure Hunt

For:

Form, shape, letter or number recognition.

Form constancy. (Rectangles are rectangles whether large or small, standing up, lying down, tipped or turned.)

Figure-ground (seeing a certain shape in spite of conflicting shapes near or overlapping).

Concepts and vocabulary of shape, space, direction and color.
Matching verbal, visual, tactile and kinesthetic stimuli.

Age: All ages. Before playing this game, children should be familiar with all the shapes (or letters) to be used in the game, through 3-D as well as 2-D experiences. (As in most activities, components should be familiar separately before they are combined.)

Materials: Chalkboard and white chalk; colored chalk is helpful but not necessary.

Directions: On the chalkboard, the teacher prepares a jumble of various large shapes (or letters, etc.) which overlap each other. With young or beginning children, use only two or three of the following basic shapes: circle, square, triangle, rectangle, diamond; and arrange the shapes with rather minimal overlapping. As children become adept, gradually increase difficulty of the puzzle by increasing (a) the number of shapes, (b) the variations in their size, (c) the degree of overlapping, (d) the overall size of the puzzle, and (e) the number of "hidden" shapes.

The teacher may say, "Who can find a square?" One child goes to the chalkboard, points to a square, then outlines it with fingertip and/or draws over it with (preferably) colored chalk. Of course, the teacher should see that every child has an equal chance at a turn that day or the next day. While pointing to or outlining the square, it is good to have the child reinforce his experience verbally by having him say, "This is a square."

Chalkboard Treasure Hunt

Note: This type of verbal reinforcement is highly desirable for *all* physical activities.

Variations: If the game is played in a very small group of one, two or three children to one adult, the teacher might say, "Sandy, outline *all* the triangles you can find with blue chalk."

The game can be a paper-and-pencil game with the puzzle prepared ahead by ditto. This is more difficult in that much more refined control of the hand is required. An advantage is that everyone in the class may perform simultaneously.

As the game palls, or with older children or younger children who are adept and secure in the game, a *little* motivation may be added by keeping score. This is best done in small groups of children who are well matched in ability, for short periods, with a minimum of comment about winning and a maximum of praise for all participants. Children may also compete against their own previous scores, with a timer or whatever.

Comments: This is one of the many games in which children can learn through watching as well as through performing. One great advantage of the game is that it can be easily changed from a very simple game through all degrees of difficulty to very challenging. Slower children may be steered to the easy parts at first; brighter children may be challenged by the more obscured "hidden" parts.

99. / Design Bingo

For:

Recognizing same or different configurations.
Visual discrimination.

Age: All ages. Young children should use very simple designs; older children's designs will increase in complexity with age and ability.

Materials: One sheet of drawing paper per child, approximately $10'' \times 14''$. (Typing paper would do in a pinch.) Fold each until there are eight rectangles.

A set of about twenty-four 3×5 cards. On the first card draw any kind of simple or complex design; on the second draw a similar design with an easily recognized difference (for younger children) or a difficult-to-recognize difference for older children. Continue until there are twelve (or so) pairs of cards, each card of a pair resembling, but differing from, the other card of the pair. Now shuffle the cards and copy any eight of the designs from the cards onto the large drawing paper sheets. Each sheet should have a different set of designs.

Design Bingo

Directions: Each child will have a drawing paper sheet, with the eight designs on it and eight paper markers before him. The teacher will flash, for a long or short period, one of the 3 × 5 cards; and each child, if he has that design on his sheet, will cover it. When a row of four designs are covered the child calls, "Bingo." When both rows are covered, the child calls, "Bingo, Bingo." Continue until every child has at least a single Bingo.

100. / Feel, Find, And Say

For:

Tactile awareness, particularly of shape and size, but also of weight and texture.
Identifying, classifying, categorizing and ordering into a series.
Attaching verbal descriptions or labels to tactile, kinesthetic and visual experiences.

Age: All ages. The variations of the game are easily adjusted from very simple to very difficult.

Materials: Certain of the following, depending on which versions of the game are being played: cardboard or plastic shapes, stencils, letters or numbers, large

Feel, Find, And Say

blocks, large beads and 3-D shapes; small sets of objects in graduated sizes, as three rectangular blocks (or boxes), balls or cars in small, medium and large sizes.

Directions:

Version 1. "Feel, Say and Draw." Children may feel objects in a box or bag, or while wearing a blindfold or behind the back. Have child feel any object which is simple enough to be drawn later on the chalkboard, such as a geometric stencil, a cut-out letter, number, etc. Child identifies the object and if correct, then draws it on the board, matching the size of the drawing as closely as possible to the size of the object.

Version 2. "Feel and Say." Child, wearing blindfold or feeling objects in a box or behind the back, tells the names of various shapes of blocks or beads (square, rectangle, etc.).

Version 3. "Feel and Describe." Child describes weight, "Which of the two objects is heavier?" or texture, "Which one is smooth?"; or unusual shape, "This object (a plastic flower) has scallops all around the edge and a sort of long stem."

Version 4. "Feel and Classify." Child tells which of two, three or four objects (as several trangles) is the larger or smaller; or child arranges in order.

Version 5. "Feel, Find and Match." "In a group of four shapes or objects (for example, two squares, one triangle and one circle), find two that are alike"; or, "In a group of three objects (two squares and one circle), find the one that's different."

Version 6. "Feel and Find Things That Go Together." "In a bag or box containing four objects, find something we write with"; or, "In two separate bags, find something we write with in the first, then find something else we write with in the second." Pairs of objects might include things we drink with (a glass, a cup); things we cut with (a pair of blunt scissors, a table knife); or things we use when we dress ourselves (a toothbrush, a comb).

26.

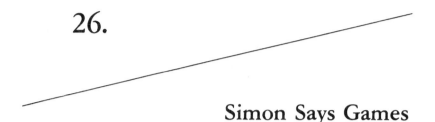

Simon Says Games

Every teacher knows the usefulness of that famous hero, Simon. Here are twenty versions of this still-sweet old chestnut. One could make up twenty more, depending on what concepts the class is working on.

How about playing Simonette Says sometimes?

101. / Simon Says Games

The game develops:

> Integration of thought and action (quick reaction to directions and signals).
> Memory (immediate).
> Agility (jumping, body movements).
> Hand coordination (thumbs up).
> Body awareness (body parts, body movements, Simon with a chair).
> Space judging (front, back, on the line; right-left practice).
> Social skills (losing a turn gracefully; following the rules).
> Vocabulary of body parts, direction and position.

Age: All ages. With young children go very slowly, and give lots of help.

Materials: A chair for each child, a chalk or string line and a chalkboard.

Versions:

> 1. Simon Says-with-a-Chair. (Put your head under the chair, etc.)

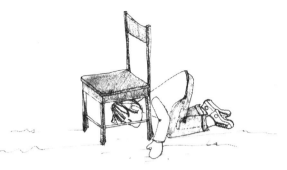

Simon Says Games

2. Simon Says Touch Body Parts. (Touch your shoulders; see Body Parts Touch, p. 32.)
3. Simon Says Body Movements (spin, jump, clap, hop).
4. Simon Says Angels-in-the-Snow. (Lying down, move right arm and leg only; see Butterflies in the Cocoon, p. 49.)
5. Simon Says Front, Back, On the Line. (Jump in front of the line.)
6. Simon Says Right, Left, Middle. (Jump to the left of the line.)
7. Simon Says With Fingers (thumbs up!).
8. Simon Says Jump Quarter Turns. (Jump a quarter turn to the left, etc.)
9. Simon Says North-East-South-West. (Everyone jump to face North.)
10. Simon Says Chalkboard Race Track. (Move your racer [chalk] to the right; see Chalkboard Games: Simon's Race Track.)
11. Simon Says Stoop; Simon Says Stand.
12. *Everyone* jump into the box (stoop), out of the box (stand). "Everyone" is the key word here. A similar version uses "Jack" as the key word. ("Jack *in* the box, Jack *out* of the box.")
13. Simon Says "On and off the Blanket." (See p. 148.)
14. Simon Says Toss a bean bag high or low; fast or slow; three feet, one yard, three meters, etc.
15. Simon Says Jump to 3 o'clock, etc.
16. Simon Says Jump to the triangle; jump to the square.
17. Simon Says Jump to the a, e, i, o, or u.
18. Simon Says Jump to the ch, sh, st blends.
19. Simon Says Jump to the four, the eight, etc.; or multiples of three, four, five, etc.
20. Simon Says Jump to words that begin with d, b, g, p, etc. (Station version: give each child a different set of three cards illustrating words that begin with d, b, etc. After each child has jumped his or her own, leave cards in place and all children move one station to the left and jump the new set of cards.)

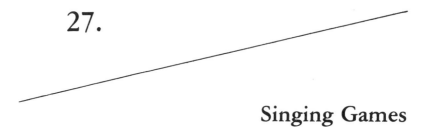

27.

Singing Games

Singing games, like dancing, are a part of every culture and have been enjoyed throughout history. They are challenging and intriguing at every age, probably because they fill a basic need for rhythmic expression.

Reading, speaking and writing are examples of school activities where rhythmic body movement and control are required. Singing *games* are even more useful than plain singing since body gestures are coordinated with auditory signals.

In addition to managing what he or she is doing, the child must think ahead of what is coming next.

102. / My Aunt Came Back

The game develops:

Coordination of up to six simultaneous body movements.
Rhythm.
Socialization, relaxation and humor.

Age: Older primary ages. Younger children may do parts.

Materials: None.

Directions: To the tune of "How Dry I Am," class echoes the leader throughout

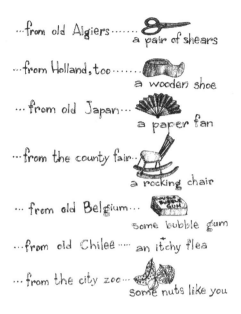

...from old Algiers······ a pair of shears

...from Holland, too······ a wooden shoe

... from old Japan··· a paper fan

...from the county fair·· a rocking chair

... from old Belgium··· some bubble gum

...from old Chilee ···· an itchy flea

...from the city zoo··· some nuts like you

My Aunt Came Back

and copies motions that accompany each verse. Once a motion is started, it is continued until the end of the game.

1. Leader: My aunt came back.

    Class echoes: My aunt came back.

    Leader: From old Algiers.

    Class: From old Algiers.

    Leader: And brought me back.

    Class: And brought me back.

    Leader: A pair of shears. (Start a cutting motion with fingers, and continue throughout song.)

    Class: A pair of shears (also starts and continues cutting).

2. . . . .from Holland, too . . . a wooden shoe. (Add the tapping of one foot.)
3. . . . .from old Japan. . . . . . a paper fan. (Add the waving of other hand.)
4. . . . .from the county fair . . a rocking chair. (Rock the upper body.)
5. . . . .from Old Belgium . . . . some bubble gum. (Purse the lips and chew.)
6. . . . .from old Chilee. . . . . an itchy flea. (Wiggle the whole body.)
7. . . . .from the city zoo . . . some nuts like you! (Everyone breaks up.)

Comments: The funniest act-out song I've come across. Adults like it too. Of course, no one can coordinate six movements well, if at all. Tell the children to do what they can; it's mostly for fun. One thing is sure: after attempting this song, the meaning of the word "coordination" becomes clear.

103. / Little Cabin In The Woods

For:

Matching verbal signals and hand gestures in a precise sequence.
Rhythm and coordination.
Body awareness.

Age: All ages. Young children will benefit from learning parts, going slower and using chalkboard reminders.

Materials: None absolutely necessary, but a chalkboard helps immensely.

Directions: Make a vertical row of pictures on the chalkboard (see illustration) to facilitate learning the correct sequence of gestures. It matters not one whit if the pictures are clumsy, except the children seem to like "dumb" pictures more than good ones.

Little Cabin in the Woods

Little Cabin In The Woods

Practice the gestures first without the song. Sing the song once (slowly) with all gestures. Repeat the song, leaving out the first line of the song but retaining the first gesture (sort of like "John Brown's Baby"). Next sing the song leaving out *two* lines of the song but retaining all gestures until finally the entire song is completely silent, but all gestures are made in order.

Variation: To make the song go faster, leave out *two* lines at a time.

Comments: Guaranteed to enchant. This song is sung and gestured in slightly different ways in different parts of the country.

It helps to mouth the words during the silent parts. Children get fairly intense rhythmic practice without realizing it.

104. / Johnny One-Hammer

For:

Isolation, strengthening and rhythmic coordination of several parts of the body, separately or simultaneously.
Matching verbal signals and motor actions.
Counting to five, forward and backward.

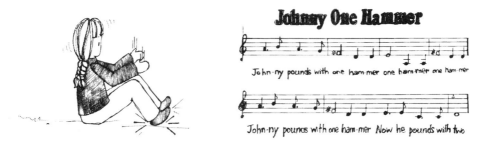

Johnny One-Hammer

Age: Kindergarten and pre-school; slow-learners of primary age.

Materials: None.

Directions: Children sit in a circle on the floor or on chairs. As the song progresses, they "pound" with (1) one fist onto the knee; (2) then two fists; (3) two fists and one foot; (4) two fists and two feet; (5) two fists, two feet, and the head. After resting a moment, the process is reversed. This is more difficult.

Instead of the name "Johnny," the names of the children in the circle can be used. The game is more strenuous than it appears and also more beneficial than we might suspect at first glance. A lot of thinking and control is required; however, the game is motivating, and children will be able to do a good job.

The very last line of the song is, "Now we're done today."

105. / Head, Shoulders, Knees And Toes, Baby

For:

Body awareness: naming parts of the body in sequence.
Rhythmic coordination of motor actions and verbal signals.

Age: The first three versions are suitable for kindergarten and pre-school. The fourth version, "Head and Shoulders, Baby" is suitable for primary ages and with some practice, for kindergartners.

Materials: None.

Directions: Children may sit on a chair or on the floor, or stand where they can watch the teacher or leader easily, and easily touch their toes. As the tunes are probably familiar, the children can sing right along the first time, matching their actions to the words and to the teacher's demonstration. The first time through, the teacher could creep his or her hands from head to shoulders, to knees, etc. and sing the song very slowly.

Version 1. To the tune of "Mulberry Bush."

a.   "Your Head (touch head) your shoulders (touch shoulders) your knees, your
        toes,
     Your head, your shoulders, your knees, your toes,
     Your head, your shoulders, your knees, your toes.
        All clap together!"

b.   The second time through, reverse the order of touching: "Your toes, your
     knees, your shoulders, your head, etc."

c.   The third (etc.) time through, have the children help you make up a verse, as:
     "Your ears, your tummy, your back, your heels, etc."
     Version 2. To the tune of "London Bridge."
     "Head and shoulders, knees and toes, knees and toes, knees and toes;
     Head and shoulders, knees and toes; My fair lady."
     Version 3. To the tune of "Tavern in the Town."
     "Head and shoulders, knees and toes, knees and toes.
     Head and shoulders, knees and toes, knees and toes.

Head & Shoulders, Baby

Head Shoul-ders, Ba-by, one, two, three

Head Shoul-ders, Ba-by, one, two, three

Head Shoul-ders, Head Shoul-ders, Head Shoul-ders, Ba-by, one, two, three.

Other verses: Shoulders - elbows
Elbows - Stomach
Stomach - Hips
Hips - Thighs
Thighs - Knees
Knees - Toes
That's all, Baby!

Head, Shoulders, Knees And Toes, Baby

And eyes, and ears, and mouth, and nose,
Head and shoulders, knees and toes! Knees and toes!"

Version 4. "Head and Shoulders, Baby!"

This jazzy little song requires a bit of practice on the part of the teacher before presenting it to the class. It's easy to get mixed up, but only the first or second time through. The teacher may use the names of as many body parts as desired, i.e., the song may run for three to ten or more verses. After the song has been sung, moving from head to shoulders, to arms, to chest to back, etc. down to the toes, it may be reversed and started again with the toes, moving up the body to ankles, legs, knees, etc.

When the song comes to "1-2-3," children may clap 1,2,3, or snap fingers, or even do a pease-porridge clap with a partner.

28.

Small Muscle Coordination

All children are clumsy with their hands for a good long time, but let's face it, some more than others. As you probably know, there are predictable physical stages in the development of the small muscles of the arms, hands and fingers which cannot and should not be forced or rushed. Yet we must make sure that every child has a great variety of opportunities to use these muscles to insure that they develop in depth and on schedule. Through appropriate easy play tasks, not only do small muscles develop properly, but the senses and mind are also stimulated. You don't have to be an expert to know exactly what tasks are appropriate for what ages; take your cues from the child. Provide a wide variety of small muscle activities that are "where he's at," and go on from there.

106. / Block Design (And Patterns)

The game develops:

Space relationships: concepts and vocabulary of direction, position, and size and color; small space judging and discrimination; seeing significant parts within a whole; a whole from parts.

Use of patterns: the beginnings of symbolism and primitive "reading"; transfer of information, a picture (or pattern) into 3-D reality and vice versa.

Sequencing, organizing, problem-solving and creating.

Eye-hand coordination.

Attention, concentration and memory.

Alert relaxation.

196

Age: The use of *very* simple block patterns starts at age three and should continue throughout early childhood in as many contexts as possible.

Materials: A set of thirty to fifty one-inch colored cube blocks per child (or enough blocks for a small group to work simultaneously).

Patterns should be same size as blocks. Some homemade cardboard patterns colored in crayon or better, with magic markers, ranging from very simple: two or three-block patterns, slowly increasing in difficulty as the child develops. A variety of 2" × 2", 3" × 3", 4" × 4", (sixteen squares) 5" × 5" (twenty-five squares) patterns is very useful.

There are dozens and dozens of types of blocks for use with or without patterns, from miniature Lego to 2' × 2' hollow wooden blocks or larger outdoor milkbox blocks. I would hope every child would have access to a wide variety of these.

Directions: Ways of using blocks and block patterns.
1. In infancy: handling, carrying, placing in rows, dumping and banging.
2. Building rows and towers both freely and later as prescribed by a pattern.
3. Copying a model (for example, a three block bridge).
4. Building on top of a cardboard pattern—start with extremely simple patterns.
5. Building on the table beside the pattern.
6. Building on the table while looking at a pattern on the wall.
7. Building vertically against a vertical pattern.
8. Covering a pattern, once mastered, and building from memory.

Block Design (And Patterns)

9. Creating own designs. Making or coloring cardboard patterns, transferring designs from blocks to paper or chalkboard and vice versa.

10. Copying the teacher's simple structure. Teacher copies the child's structure; teacher makes a deliberate change in structure to see if child can catch it and vice versa.

11. Experiment with all types of free-form patterns: circular, diagonal, vertical and combinations of these.

12. Sometimes (especially with a slow learner) it is helpful for the teacher to share the work with a child.

Suggestions: For language and vocabulary, verbalize as you go.

There are many good ways of working a block design. I do not insist that a child do it the way I would (i.e., build from left to right, from top down, etc.). I would like her to know that there are many ways of organizing space, and of attacking a problem (from the outside in, from the center out, etc.); if a child has *no* systematic way of starting to work a pattern, I give instruction freely. Other factors being equal, linear patterns should be worked left to right.

The benefits of block design are so numerous that I consider block-and-patterns one of the top educational toys. Like many of our basic toys and equipment, *anything* a child does with blocks and patterns is useful.

The ideal way to use blocks is in a 1:1 relationship with an adult providing verbal feedback. These instructions apply to beads and pegs too.

107. / Peg Boards And Rubber Bands

For:

All of the benefits of block designs and patterns. (See previous game.)
Also, a different and somewhat higher level of fine muscle coordination and a different type of creativity.

Age: All ages. Very young children may do more free play than pattern following.

Materials: For a single child, two pegboards (one for a model), two sets of colored rubber bands and colored pegs. For very young children, the pegs should be large to start, switching to smaller ones as skills are acquired.

For a class, several sets should be made or purchased so a group can work simultaneously if desired.

Directions: Follow the general sequence of activities as given for block designs, moving from (1) completely unstructured play (and no rubber bands) to (2) copy-

Peg Boards And Rubber Bands

ing a very simple model (pegs only), to (3) free play adding rubber bands any old way, to (4) copying a simple model with one or two rubber bands added to a very simple peg arrangement; (5) add more rubber bands to the model, (6) use simple cardboard patterns (life-size pictures) and increase difficulty of patterns. Some patterns are perforated and are placed and worked right on top of the pegboard. Over the years, slowly move to (7) making up or coloring one's own patterns on the pegboard, chalkboard or on paper, and (8) having the child transfer his own pattern to another model, or chalkboard, or paper, and vice versa.

Variations:

1. Paint a large pegboard with blackboard paint and add chalk patterns; pegboard should be about $12'' \times 12''$.
2. For dexterity older children might race a timer or race each other working a familiar pattern. Be sure the child is working under slight pressure only.
3. Fasten a square of onion skin or tissue paper to the pegboard with masking tape. Punch through the paper with a peg, making a row of holes or a design. A colored pattern might be drawn onto the paper before fastening it to the pegboard.

108. / Suspendable Ball

For:

Near and far focus of the eyes; tracking.

Rhythmic coordination of both hands together or either hand separately, guided by the eyes.

Numbers and counting.

Suspendable Ball

Age: All ages.

Materials: A wiffle ball suspended from ceiling or doorway by a thin but strong rope, preferably nylon. A sturdy rolling pin, preferably with three different colored stripes painted or taped on. Helpful but not necessary: other small paddles to hit the ball with, as a ping-pong paddle, a toy plastic badminton racquet, etc.

Directions: The ball should be fastened securely to doorway or ceiling by a string that will take considerable abuse. The rolling pin will hopefully not fall apart if dropped. The object of the game is to hold the rolling pin with both hands and bat the wiffle ball as many times as possible before missing. If the teacher or an aide can count as the child pops the ball, the child will be motivated to continue longer.

Variations:
1. Stripes on the rolling pin will enable the child to hit the ball in a pattern: hit once on the red stripe, once on the green stripe, once on the blue stripe; continue to repeat this pattern. Complicated patterns may be worked out.
2. Children may use one hand only with the rolling pin, a ping-pong paddle or a racquet.
3. If there is space and if the rope is strong, children may practice hitting with a plastic baseball bat.
4. The suspendable ball game may be alternated with some other exercise that is appropriate for the child to practice. "To earn ten swings at the suspendable ball, you have to hop on your right foot ten times (or do five

sit-ups, etc.)." With this approach, the suspendable ball is used as an operant to get the child to practice something that is perhaps difficult or dull, but still necessary and useful.

5. For a change, the suspendable ball may be raised high so that the child must jump to hit the ball with an open hand or paddle. Perhaps there could be several balls hung at varying heights for varying sized children to jump and hit.

6. Fasten a paper clown face or other target on the side of the doorway or wall, and let children hit the ball against this target.

When the children tire of the suspendable ball, it should be removed and kept out of sight for a few weeks.

109. / Punch Out

For:

Manual dexterity.
Form recognition (basic shapes, designs, letters, numbers, etc.).

Age: All ages.

Punch Out

Materials: A small rectangle of thin carpet, about twelve by fifteen inches; plain paper; a stylus made of a single-pointed corn-on-the-cob holder, or an old ball-point pen. Shallow styrofoam supermarket meat trays.

Directions: With pencil, the teacher draws one or more large geometric designs on a sheet of paper. Place the paper on top of the rectangle of carpet. The paper may be anchored with masking tape if desired. Using the pointed stylus, the child punches holes in the paper along the pencil lines, about every one-fourth inch. The design then may or may not be torn out along the punched lines. If several designs have been torn out, these can be fitted back in, making a simple puzzle.

Variations:

1. The child may copy a design from a picture model or make up his own.
2. Designs may be punched onto the bottoms of foam-plastic grocery store meat trays.

Comments: Children of all ages, even those who are ordinarily impatient with fine motor dexterity games, enjoy this method of tracing designs.

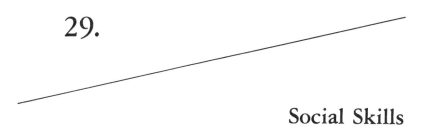

29.

Social Skills

Of all the games, children like the social ones best, and for good reason: the social games are those with group interaction and a few very simple rules of give and take (or you might say with cooperation and sometimes gentle competition). These are also the games where if you're not careful, you may have too much frustration and tears, or too little challenge resulting in boredom, or too much excitement resulting in overstimulation and misbehavior.

I think it's a good idea to precede each game of low organization with a brief discussion of the "booby traps" within the game: the parts that may be frustrating or otherwise difficult. Also, if children are told that all who play the game are winners because they're learning new skills and their bodies are getting stronger, they not only hear that, but they are greatly relieved.

110. / The Giants And The Dragons

The game develops:

> Listening skills.
> Social skills: tagging gently, getting caught and the beginning of teamwork.
> Running, chasing.
> Following a sequence of directions.

Age: All ages. Young children will need to be led through the first game.

The Giants And The Dragons

Materials: Two ropes, string or chalk line markers.

Directions: May be played indoors or out. Half of the children stand behind a boundary line on one side of the room (the giants in their castle). Half are behind an opposite boundary line about fifteen to twenty feet away (the dragons in their cave). Giants may not step into dragons' cave, and dragons may not cross into giants' castle.

When the teacher gives the signal to start, giants tip-toe toward the dragon's cave; dragons get ready to chase on a signal. When the giants have come very close, the teacher gives the run signal. "The Dragons are coming!" Giants run home, dragons run after them and try to tag them gently (but do not try to stop them).

Any giants who are tagged become dragons (chasers); hence, they are still active in the game.

Comments: A few simple precautions will keep the game from getting out of hand. Talk over the simple rules and "bobby traps" (possible frustrations), i.e., tag gently; don't push, grab or tackle; don't run until you hear the signal, etc. Anyone who forgets and grabs or tackles must lose a turn.

This is one of the simplest of team games; there are no losers. It sends the children into squeals of delight. Follow with a quiet game.

111. / Frogs And Pollywogs

For:

Following simple rules and a sequence of directions.

Social give and take: taking turns, tagging, getting caught, changing roles and contributing to group enjoyment.

Quick reaction and simple agility skills: reaching, dodging and ducking.

Age: All ages.

Materials: Chairs.

Directions: Discuss the differences between frogs and baby pollywogs (or tadpoles), i.e., pollywogs gradually develop legs as they change into frogs; frogs may live out of water, etc.

Explain the rules and emphasize for pollywogs: (1) no fair getting caught deliberately (you lose a turn), (2) it's part of the fun to get caught; and for frogs: (1) no fair standing up, (2) no fair hitting.

The game: Construct an instant island in the center of the room (one chair) with a great big frog (Grandma or Grandpa Frog) on it. Pick a Child #1 who must sit on the chair and catch (touch gently) as many pollywogs (her classmates) as she can as they swim by. Child #1 may reach in any direction but *must be sitting in contact with the chair* at all times (may not stand up). As pollywogs are caught, they change into frogs and adding chairs, join Child #1 on the island helping tag remaining pollywogs. Continue until all pollywogs are caught.

But: Also place two (or more) "big rocks" (chairs) near the island (about six feet away) with a channel running between island and rocks. Pretend that as the tide goes out, the channel of water gets narrower and narrower (as the game goes on, the teacher moves the "rocks" in closer and closer to the island) until the Grandma Frog and her helpers can catch every one of the pollywogs.

Frogs And Pollywogs

This game is dearly loved by every child and is often requested. It is an excellent socializer because it is hilarious, everyone gets caught, and there are no losers—everyone continues to play until the end.

Comments: Don't expect this game to go too well the first time. There may be errors of judgment or overstimulation and minor frustrations which will yield quickly to correction as teacher and children learn the ropes; but it is worth the effort. Minimize (or forget) praise for the last child caught and maximize praise for all the players and their contribution to the fun. If children tire or become overstimulated, move the "rocks" in quickly so the game can be ended. Children will learn on their own that a longer game results from reasonable self-control.

112. / Ten Trips

For:

Eye-hand coordination; practicing various object handling skills.
Quick reactions, attention, alertness and aim.
Helping teammates pass the ball quickly.

Age: Primary grades. Younger children may play an easier, slower version of the game.

Ten Trips

Materials: A playground ball for each group of five or six children.

Directions: Divide the class into several teams of about five or six children each; each team stands in a circle. Standing close makes the game easier, and standing farther apart makes it more challenging. Designate an adult aid or a dependable child to be the leader of each team. The balls are passed around each circle quickly upon the signal "go." Each time the ball passes through the leader's hands, he or she counts one trip. The first team to complete ten trips around the circle with the ball raises arms silently to signal they are finished. That team gets one point. In the next round of the game, all teams enlarge their circles, and this time they will toss the ball around.

Variations: The ball may be rolled, tossed high, bounced, thrown with the right hand only, etc. Young children may play a shorter version, Five Trips.

Comments: If one team is losing consistently, exchange some members for a better balance.

113. / Midnight

For:

> Following easy rules and a sequence of steps to make a simply organized game.
>
> Social give-and-take and sportsmanship: how to get caught gracefully, tag gently, change roles, chase and be chased.
>
> Quick reaction to verbal signal.

Age: All ages. Young children will require more active guiding through the game at first.

Materials: None. Ropes or chalk lines to mark two boundaries are very helpful.

Directions: Mark two boundary lines at opposite ends of the room, or about thirty to forty feet apart outdoors. One line marks the foxes' den, the other the geese's pen. It is important for the teacher to emphasize that the fox(es) will be chasing the geese, and that the foxes must tag gently, touching the geese on the arm or shoulder. No grabbing or holding is permitted. It is not necessary for the foxes to *stop* the geese. Discuss the fact that if you are caught, you are *not* out of the game, you only change roles.

One or more foxes stands inside the foxes' boundary line. All the geese advance slowly from their pen toward the foxes, asking from time to time, "Mr.

Midnight

Fox, what time is it?" The fox replies, "It's 8 o'clock," or "It's two o'clock," etc. After several such interchanges, the fox may suddenly reply, "It's midnight!" This is the signal for the geese to run back to their pen, and for the fox(es) to chase and attempt to tag them. Any geese who are tagged become foxes and help chase and tag.

Comments: There are several things the teacher can do to make sure the game does not become wild or rough. He or she can warn that any children who tag by holding must lose a turn. Or the teacher may start the game with only a few children as demonstrators, adding more after each chase. A slow-motion demonstration may help, demonstrating how to tag. In any case, the teacher should supervise fairly actively the first time through, adapting the rules as the class needs until the children become familiar with the idea of the game, which is really quite simple. It is guaranteed to become a favorite.

30.

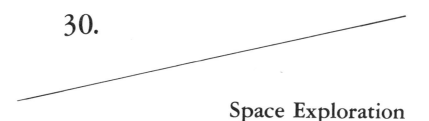

Space Exploration

Once a child develops some (hopefully a lot of) body awareness and a feeling of the areas on and within his body, he begins to apply this largely unconscious knowledge to the world outside of and immediately surrounding his body. Gradually a feeling for the predictability, the dimensions and the coordinates of space, is extended farther and farther from the child's body. He is able to make judgments as to distances, spaces, shapes and sizes relating to himself and an object, and between two or more objects "out there" away from him. He sees how the world all hangs together space-wise.

Games which call attention to distances and/or size and/or direction, whether one-fourth inch or four hundred yards or anything in between, add to the child's space information bank.

114. / Rope Obstacle Course

The game develops:

Awareness of small and large distances by crawling, walking, hopping and jumping through and over various sized spaces.
Ability to follow directions and visual signals.
Balance, agility, coordination and strength.
Vocabulary of body parts, positions, distances, directions, etc.

Rope Shapes II

Age: All ages. Ropes may be arranged into extremely easy or extremely difficult positions.

Materials: A variety of short ropes and/or strings, a tom-tom and one or two longer ropes or strings.

Directions: Arrange ropes and/or strings into as many obstacles as possible or convenient.
1. Some at various heights to jump over. (Tie loosely for safety.)
2. Some to crawl under, or crawl between.
3. Curved or zig-zag ropes to walk beside or on.
4. Parallel ropes to walk like a path, requiring heel-toe balance.
5. Parallel ropes on the floor to jump over or across.
6. Rope circles to hop through.
7. Lengthwise parallel ropes to crawl along, or "swim" along.

Variations:
1. Make up your own obstacles possibly adding animal walk pictures as traffic signs, tables, chalk marks, etc.
2. On a tom-tom signal, everyone freeze, and/or move backward. (See Improvised Obstacle Courses, p. 134.)

115. / Rope Shapes II

For:

Fitting the body into a given space in different ways (transferring inner space information to outer spaces).

Following a series of directions.
Vocabulary of body parts, positions, words of space and place.
Integrating words, actions, observations and feelings.

Age: All ages.

Materials: A six- or preferably seven-foot rope for each child; a tom-tom.

Directions: Each child makes a circle "house" in which she sits without touching the rope with body or clothing; kneels in; stoops in; lies down in (on back); (on side).

Variations:

1. Each child makes some shape other than a circle, which she fits into in various ways. Leaving her rope in position on the floor, on a tom-tom signal, she moves to the right and fits into a new shape.
2. Children might go for a space walk, walking freely in the room among, but not in any of the shapes on the floor. Suddenly there's a signal, "Everyone jump into a triangle." (See Rope Shapes I, p. 182, and Space Walk, p. 111.)
3. Make larger and larger shapes out of combined ropes; several children may fit into one shape.

Rope Obstacle Course

116. / Geiger Counter

For:

Interpreting auditory clues to solve a directional, spatial problem.
Understanding the relationship between frequency of auditory clues (clapping) and distance (closer).
Social skills: cooperating to help a classmate find a hidden object.

Age: Kindergarten and primary grades.

Geiger Counter

Materials: A chalkboard eraser or any similarly sized object.

Directions: This is a clever and more difficult version of the game of "Hot and Cold." Child #1 hides his eyes or steps out of the room; Child #2 hides the eraser anywhere in the room so that part or all of it is visible. Child #1 returns to the group and begins to walk around the room, searching for the hidden eraser. If he moves into the general area where the eraser is hidden, the rest of the children begin to clap slowly and softly. As Child #1 gets closer to the eraser, the other children clap somewhat faster and louder. When Child #1 gets very close, the class claps very fast and very loud. If at any time Child #1 moves away from the eraser, the clapping diminishes. Both the child who is "It" *and* the clapping children learn to gauge auditory clues for the purpose of mental planning and physical action. If the auditory clues are interpreted correctly, there is a reinforcing reward: the object is found. If the object is not found within some specified time limit, Child #1 may be given increasingly broad hints as to where the object is.

Comments: The teacher may and should use this game for explaining and emphasizing the thinking strategy involved in guiding the eyes and body by the frequency and intensity of the claps. The teacher might, for example, take the first turn hunting for the eraser and verbalize aloud his or her thoughts while moving around the room, "I don't hear any claps here, so I'd better move somewhere else. Oh, I hear a few slow claps, I'm getting closer. I'm hearing many more claps now, so I'll stay in this general area and hunt more closely, etc."

117. / Bean Bag Throw And Follow

For:

Combining visual and kinesthetic spatial information.
Acting out the words: over, under, between, high and low, left and right.
Object handling and aim.

Age: All ages. Distances and targets may be made very easy or very difficult according to age.

Bean Bag Throw And Follow

Materials: A bean bag for each child. One or two long ropes; several hoops or trays.

Directions: The object is for the child to (1) throw a bean bag *over* a rope (or *between* two ropes stretched across the room), (2) hit a gigantic target (as one or several hoops) and (3) with his body, follow the path of the bean bag by stepping over the rope and picking up his own bean bag, and (4) returning to the end of the line of children.

Variations: Children may throw *under* a rope or *between* two "goal posts" (chairs). There may be two stations or more; for example, first throw *over* a rope and retrieve bean bag, then move to next station where children throw *under* a rope and retrieve, then return to end of line. To make the target both easy for inadept children while also challenging for adept ones, place a metal tray inside the hoop (one or more); on the tray, stand a bowling pin or milk carton. Children may receive one point for hitting inside the hoop, two points for hitting the tray, and three points for hitting the bowling pin. Left or right variations could be added, for example, "Throw your bean bag to the left hoop, go around the left end to retrieve it, pick the bean bag up with your left hand."

31.

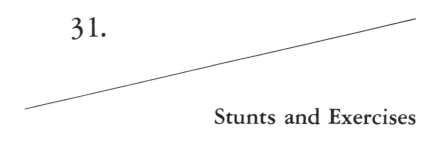

Stunts and Exercises

Stunts have strong appeal for children: they give confidence and develop strength, balance, coordination and flexibility. There are few activities which so dramatically call attention to precise awareness and differentiation of the body parts. Also they are very portable; children can practice them at home and show them off a little. They lend themselves to self-competition.

It is better in many ways for a child to be able to do twenty simple stunts than two or three hard ones. We want children to get hooked on success and become aware of the versatility of their bodies.

118. / Twenty-Five Easy Stunts

The game develops:

Balance, coordination, strength and flexibility.
Body awareness in various spaces and positions.
Self-confidence.
Vocabulary of body parts, position, space and direction.
Combining visual, verbal and kinesthetic information.

Age: All ages will be able to do most of these stunts.

Materials: A mat or rug is helpful. Number three requires a bean bag; number twenty-four requires a large ball.

215

Directions: Do only two or three or so until all are learned. Keep practice time short, and praise willingness to try as well as achievement. A checklist, if used tactfully, is motivating. Avoid comparing children; encourage *self*-competition.

Twenty-five Easy Stunts
1. Broad jump: both standing and running.
2. Jump and clap hands.
3. Jump and spin.
4. Jump with bean bag held between knees or ankles.
5. Hop, each foot (by age four and one-half); preferred foot (by age three and one-half).
6. Balance on each foot to count of five seconds (by age six: fifteen seconds).
7. Indian stand: stand on line, heel to toe (by age five: eight seconds).
8. Walk toes in (pigeon walk); toes out (clown walk).
9. Scissor jump: advance, alternating feet apart, then together.
10. Backward jump, sideways jump (feet together).
11. Balance on toes (by age five: ten seconds).
12. Gallop, while slapping hip. Skip (age five).
13. Windmill: rotate arms various ways, forward, back and alternating.
14. Toe-touch: with stiff knees, if possible; hold three seconds.
15. Cradle: sit, grasp knees, rock on back and up to sitting.

Twenty-Five Easy Stunts

16. Bicycle: lie on back; make circles in air with feet.
17. Human rocker: on stomach, raise head, arms, legs and hold or rock.
18. Flag pole: lie on side, lift one leg and wave foot.
19. Blast-off: slowly lower body to stoop position, counting ten-nine-eight etc. Jump up on "Blast-off!"
20. Log roll: keep body straight, arms overhead.
21. Egg sit: sit, grasp knees, lift feet slightly, hold.
22. Somersault: forward, backward.
23. Overhead toe-touch: lie on back, raise legs until one or both toes touch floor behind head, hold.
24. Throw, bounce, catch a large rubber ball (various ways).
25. Wall head stand: easier than it appears, but give help at first. Place top of head about four inches from wall, use hands as brace and lift legs up until feet rest against wall. Hold a few seconds.

Comments: This stunt list can be helpful in spotting and helping children with motor problems. If a child cannot do many, try to increase his or her physical activity in general, as well as specific skills in stunts.

119. / Swimming Pool (Or Disneyland)

For:

> Social skills: taking turns, learning to move up a line; low-key "performance" before a group; appreciation of own and others' efforts.
> Body awareness: comparative feedback, both in watching and in doing the various parts of the game.
> Space judging, especially in doing the "semaphores."
> Responding to visual signals, use of a code (symbols).
> Listening: extending attention span.
> Repeating a sequence and following simple rules.

Age: All ages. Young children may do a simplified version and jump from lower heights. (Not more than six or eight children should play at one time, or the game will be overly long.)

Materials: A strong table about two and a half feet high to jump from; a gym mat to jump onto, though an old mattress, or several layers of rugs or old blankets would do; chairs for a train.

Directions: Game may be easily shortened or simplified.

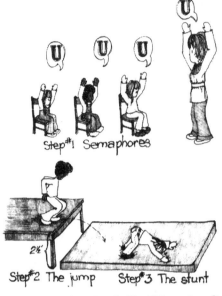

Swimming Pool (Or Disneyland)

1. Arrange your Disneyland Part as follows: a table (diving board) at one end of a mat (the pool) and a row of chairs beside the mat (the train).

2. Emphasize the correct way to jump: "Bend knees for spring; let your arms help give you lift and balance; and absorb the shock by letting knees bend as you land on feet." The teacher must emphasize repeatedly, "Be careful never to land on your knees. After landing, use hands to lean on, if needed to maintain balance."

3. Explain the rules and the sequence: (a) children start by sitting in the train; (b) children will imitate the teacher's "semaphore" arm signals. For example, Child #1's name is Sue. Teacher says "S" and signals a finger to his lips. The children do the same. Next he gives the U signal, arms out and up, something like a U. All children imitate. "E": teacher points both arms to the side. Children imitate. Then Sue leaves the train and climbs up onto the table; (c) Sue jumps to the mat, then does a stunt, e.g., a somersault; (d) other children move up one chair in the train of chairs; (e) Sue takes the last chair. When each child has had a turn, game is ended.

Variations and comments:

1. "Swimming Pool" is really a way of combining several valuable activities into one game. Use your imagination to change it any way you wish.

2. Children may all do the same stunt, all do different stunts, think up their own, or pick from a stack of stunt cards.

3. Each child should have the option of jumping from a lower height if he or she wishes. Without being moralistic, this may be a good time to point out that it may take more courage for some children to jump from a low platform than for others to jump from a high one.

4. As children increase in jumping skill, add a firmly braced chair to the table top to add height.

5. If a child loses balance or sprawls on landing, he probably needs to jump from a lower platform for a while.

6. Just *what* arm signals you use are unimportant; sometimes the signals resemble the letters of the alphabet, but this is not mandatory.

120. / Basic Body Exercises and Calisthenics

For:

Strength, coordination, flexibility and agility.
Rhythmic repetition.
Body awareness: isolation of parts and precise control of body.

Age: All; but the younger the child, the more moderate should be the routine.

Materials: A jump rope for each child to make a "house" is helpful in spacing young children. Mats of any kind (or a carpeted floor) are also desirable.

Introductory comments: Most early childhood and physical educators frown (correctly) on the use of physical drills in the education of the pre-schooler or early primary-aged child. However, calisthenics can be extremely beneficial *if* (1) boring drills are avoided, (2) the exercises are used as a very brief daily warm-up activity of not over two minutes total length, (3) they are used as a supplement to other strenuous activities (as four minutes total time twice a week), and/or for (4) corrective work with a particularly weak or discoordinated child (for a total of six or seven minutes at a time, individually supervised and assisted; if (5) exercises are varied from day to day, (6) there are no more than five repetitions of any one exercise, and (7) perhaps more importantly, the teacher often incorporates the exercises into a story or game-like context. (See suggestions which follow.)

This is quite a big order, but it can be done and benefits will be great.

The fact is that there are many children who need more intensive fitness training than can be obtained in regular children's physical games. Often these poorly conditioned children sit during recess or free time and hang back or melt into the woodwork during game time. Quite unconsciously, they have dozens of ways of passively resisting physical activity. A vicious circle of avoidance and weakness is set up. The astute teacher will not settle for this and hopefully, through constant motivation and positive reinforcement, will build up the child's physical adequacy and self-esteem. This is a big responsibility for the teacher, but one consolation is that the poorer the child's physical condition, the more dramatic are the benefits.

Following are some examples of basic exercises which will include work on (1) the trunk (back, abdominal, and chest) muscles; (2) arm and shoulder muscles; and (3) hip and leg muscles. An endless variety of exercises can be obtained in exercise books or elementary physical education books, for example, *Dynamic Physical Education for Elementary School Children*, Dauer and Pangrazi, Burgess Publishing Company, Minneapolis, 1975 and *How to Keep Your Child Fit from Birth to Six*, Bonnie Prudden, Harper and Row, New York, 1964.

Examples of exercises from which to choose: (Repeat each about five times.)

1. (Whole body stretch) Side-bends: child's arms are extended overhead, legs are apart. With both arms, child reaches as far as possible to left, then to right.
2. (Whole body stretch) Toe-touches: child's legs should be essentially straight but knees are not rigidly pushed back into locked position. Child should reach toward the toes as far as possible, gently extending his reach over days and weeks. On the upswing, child reaches toward the ceiling and leans back.
3. Easy sit-ups (primarily for abdomen and trunk): child lies on back with knees slightly bent. Child's hands rest on the thighs. Child lifts head first, then shoulders and then back, curling to upright seated position. If this is impossible, child may grasp the cloth of his trousers or pull on a jump rope fastened nearby, until a little more strength is gained.
4. Modified push-ups, regular push-ups, or let-downs (primarily for arms and chest): child supports body on hands and toes (or modified: hands and

Basic Body Exercises and Calisthenics

knees). Child lowers and raises body in a straight line a few times. If necessary, child only *lowers* body slowly and gets back up any way possible.

5. Side leg-lift (primarily for hips): child lies on side in a straight line, with one arm extended under the head. Child lifts one leg at a time as high as possible and lowers it.

6. Back-arch (for back strength): lying on stomach with arms at sides, child lifts head, shoulders and legs. Lower and repeat.

7. Leg lifts: lying on back, child lifts both legs up to perpendicular position then lowers. If necessary, child may lift one leg at a time until strength is built up.

8. (For heart and lung strength): Running in place, running laps, or jumping jacks.

Ways for making calisthenics interesting and fun:

1. Encourage the best performance from each child that is within his or her reach. This may include accepting even *poor* performances from poorly conditioned children until strength is built up. Reinforce positively every small effort from these children.

2. Show children pictures from exercise books.

3. Do the exercises with the children if at all possible.

4. Use 5 × 7 cards with simple stick figure sketches as visual reminders.

5. Let each child make a "house" from a circle of jump rope on the floor. Allow children to change to a new house for each exercise.

6. Put a different stick-figure card in each circle and let children move from station to station.

7. Let the calisthenic period precede a favorite game.

8. Keep the calisthenic routine very brief and varied.

9. Tell the children what each exercise is good for. ("This will increase your arm strength and help you throw the ball farther.")

10. Tell children that calisthenics will gradually increase health, good looks, and sports and game abilities. (They will.)

11. Let a different child (children) be the leader(s) each day.

12. When possible, let children work in pairs; for example, sit-ups can be a partner rowing activity.

13. Make up a story to go along with exercises. The story need not be clever. An example: "Pretend you're Uncle Wiggly, waking up from a nap (sit-ups); or nibbling some lettuce (push-ups); or exercising his tired old legs (leg-lifts).

14. Play a Simon Says type of activity: "Children, I'm going to try to trick you during our toe touches. I'll count and you touch your toes with each count. Sometimes I'll count fast and sometimes slowly; see if you can

stay with me. Suddenly I may stop counting altogether; then see if you can freeze in mid air."

15. Keep a simple record for each child for the purpose of *self*-competition.

16. Part of the time, allow the child to choose what exercises he wants to do, and/or whether he wants to do the easy or hard version. (Such choice is more suitable to individual or very small group work.)

121. / I'll Chase You 'Round The Mountain

For:

Strength and agility, balance and coordination.
Practicing various locomotor patterns: hops, jumps, runs, walks, crawls, any or all animal walks, etc.

Age: All ages.

I'll Chase You Round The Mountain

Materials: A table, chair or other large object to represent the mountain.

Directions: Children stand on a starting line. The "mountain," table or chair is placed about fifteen feet away. The teacher begins to sing the "Mountain Song." This is the signal for the children to start around the mountain in whatever locomotor pattern has been agreed upon. Actually, there is no chasing, nor is the game a race to see who gets home first; the object is for all children to be able to move around the mountain and return to their exact home (starting) places before the music runs out. The teacher may pace his or her singing so that most (or in the case of young children, all) children have time to get home. Older children; who perhaps need a bit of competition to keep the game interesting, could receive a strike for *not* getting home on time, and three strikes means the loss of one turn. The song may be repeated five, six, seven times—whatever the traffic will bear, each time using a different locomotor pattern.

Comments: The children will get caught up in the fun of trying to get home in time and will happily and strenuously exert themselves, obtaining quite a good workout in a short time. The game could be made into a race if the teacher wishes.

32.

Tactile Games

Children in our culture depend heavily on sight and sound for learning. However, when *all* senses are working well, learning experiences are facilitated and deepened.

The ability to learn through the tactile sense is a vital skill for young children to have.

122. / Touch By Ten

The game develops:

The sense of touch.
Concepts and the language of size, shape, texture and color.

Age: First-graders, kindergartners and pre-schoolers.

Materials: The ordinary objects in the classroom.

Directions: The teacher or leader says, "Find and touch something smooth in the room by the time I count to ten. When you find something, put your finger on it and freeze it there. Ready, go! 1-2-3-4-5-6-7-8-9-10! Now let's see what you've found. George, what did you find? A door knob, good. Jane found what? A plastic cup. Bob is touching the sink; Linda, the table top, etc."

"Now let's find something *rough* by the count of 10" (or soft, fuzzy, sharp, round, big, little, large, etc.).

Touch By Ten

Variations: Touch colors by ten, shapes ("anything rectangular, etc.").

Team version: Divide class into teams of four. When the leader says "Go" all children run to touch something, then return to team line. First team back wins a point.

123. / Tactile Add-Ons

For:

> Developing awareness and depth of the tactile sense.
> Matching tactile information with visual and verbal information.
> Increasing the vocabulary of textures, shapes, sizes, materials as well as place, position, color.
> Memory for a series of objects.

Age: All ages. Young children may play a shorter version.

Materials: The ordinary objects in the classroom.

Directions: Let's say the class is studying rectangles. The children are at the point of needing to transfer the concepts of a chalkboard or stencil rectangle to real-life objects and vice versa, i.e., they're looking for rectangles in the room. Child #1 starts by finding a rectangle, say a book; he touches it and returns to his seat. Child #2 touches the book, and adds-on her rectangle—the cupboard door;

she touches it (perhaps outlines it with a finger) and sits down. Child #3 touches book, door, and adds another rectangular object: a table top. Child #4 touches book, door, table top and adds calendar. Continue as far as children are able, perhaps to six or seven items.

Variations: Play the game using various shapes, textures, sizes and materials (or a combination).

Play the game using colors or places (high things, low things).

Touch 1 – Book   Touch 2 – Cupboard door

Touch 3 – Table top   Touch 4 – Calendar

Tactile Add-Ons

Comments: The add-on idea is a very versatile and an instant way to make other learning experiences into memory games. Some examples include rhyming word add-ons and letters-that-begin-with-d add-ons. It can be played outdoors or in, in the swimming pool (different strokes), on the trampoline (various jumps), or in a car (categories of words).

124. / Tactile Telephone

For:

Tactile awareness.
Shape recognition: comparison of tactile and visual information.
Concepts and language of direction, right and left shapes, size, etc.

Age: The game may be made easy or difficult by using simple or complex designs.

Tactile Telephone

Materials: A chalkboard (or paper and pencils).

Directions: Children sit in a long line (or two or more lines) with each child facing the back of the child in front of him. Instead of sending a telephone message verbally, the message (a design) will be sent by touch. The teacher starts a design message by drawing on the back of the last child in (each) line, and the design is passed up the line. The child nearest the front puts the tactile message he has received onto the chalkboard. Discrepancies between what message was started and what message finished are noted by the class.

Note that it is suggested that the teacher start all designs while the children are learning the game. It is important that the designs be easy enough for *all* the children, for example, the basic shapes. Letters or numbers might be used for older children. After children are familiar with the game, they may take turns as starters.

Comments: The game provides a natural opportunity for enlarging the vocabulary of directional words. Paradoxically, increasing tactile awareness also increases visual awareness.

125. / Tactile Pictures

For:

Integrating, organizing and visualizing tactile information.

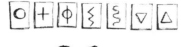

Tactile Pictures

Transferring tactile to visual information.
Verbalizing about direction, shape, size, etc.
Immediate memory.

Age: There is an easy version for young children; more difficult versions for older ones. The game is easily adjusted from extremely easy to extremely difficult, by varying the complexity of the designs.

Materials: A set of 5 × 7 cards, with any simple designs drawn on them (preferably graduated in difficulty). About ten cards are needed, although all may not be used at once. A chalk and chalkboard are needed for the third version, although paper and pencil could be used.

Directions: Children learn both from watching other children perform and by doing the game themselves. Prop the cards on a chalkboard ledge or anywhere they are easily visible to the whole group.

Version 1. Child #1 sits near and looking at the cards with other children seated in a line or semi-circle behind him. With his fingertip, Child #2 "draws" any one of the designs onto the back of Child #1. Child #1 identifies which of the designs was drawn by pointing to the proper card.

Version 2. As above, but put the cards on a table out of sight of Child #1. After he has felt the design drawn by Child #2, child #1 then goes to the table and selects the design that was drawn on his back.

Version 3. After receiving the tactile message, Child #1 goes to the chalkboard and draws the design on the board.

Comments: Discrepancies between the message sent and the message received should be pointed out tactfully.

Very young children might be asked to discriminate among only two or three simple and/or dissimilar designs. Older children might be expected to discriminate among many, complex, and/or similar designs. Trial and error will enable the teacher quickly to find the best level for his or her class.

33.

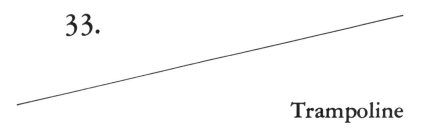

Trampoline

I have a long-lasting love affair with trampolines. This is one type of equipment with which *anything* the child does is of benefit, no matter how gently, how simply or how cleverly it is used. The trampoline provides benefits of endurance, coordination, balance and confidence. The trampoline is friendly to young and old, the handicapped or athletically gifted child. Concepts of space, size, distance, direction, time, numbers, clock positions and the language that accompany these, all can be worked into trampoline activities. Rebound stunts (the knee-drop, etc.) are fine for the older child, but this is only one of many uses of the tranpoline.

Yes, trampolines *are* expensive; yes, with a very few precautions, they are safe. But don't just stand there. Have a rummage sale or fish fry and get your school one. Consider a pit type trampoline for extra safety.

126. / Jump the Rising Stick

The game develops:

Rhythmic, overall body coordination and strength.
Endurance (cardiovascular).
Balance in new relationships to gravity.
Body awareness and confidence.
Direction-space-time concepts and language; side to side, over; front and
    back, high and low, vertical and horizontal; space-time relationships:
    high = longer time between jumps, low = shorter time, etc.
Visual steering.

229

Jump The Rising Stick

Age: All ages.

Materials: A trampoline and a four-foot pole or stick.

Directions: The teacher holds the pole across, and as close as possible to the trampoline bed. Child practices stepping over it, then jumping across it. After a few jumps, the teacher says, "Now I'm going to raise the pole just a little bit"; raise the pole only one inch and let the child jump over it. Gradually increase the height of the pole, by inches or half-inches. If the child encounters difficulty decrease the pole height.

Comments: "Jump the Rising Stick" is one of the easiest but most useful trampoline activities for any age child. So that there is maximum opportunity for turns, trampoline play should be done in small groups (of two to four children). As the child understands the game, the teacher should let the *child* indicate where she wants the pole, "Shall I raise the pole? How much? Shall I lower the pole? How much?" Our goal is not so much high jumping as (1) motivation to enjoy jumping, and (2) height concepts.

Variations: Add small weights to arm(s) or leg(s).

127. / How Many Ways

For:

All of the benefits listed under the previous game ("Jump the Rising Stick"). Plus: creativity and more extensive language development; memory.

How Many Ways

Age: All ages.

Materials: Only the trampoline is needed, but a beach or playground size ball, a bean bag, a rope (short and/or long), masking tape or chalk all lend themselves to making up trampoline activities.

Directions: The teacher asks any of the questions below. The child jumps and (hopefully, but not necessarily) verbalizes the answer. Somewhat more difficult: child verbalizes first, then demonstrates the answer.

"How many ways can you move on the trampoline?"

Walking, sit and bounce, hands and knees, etc., lying down, somersault.

Jump: feet apart, together or alternating.

Forward, backward, sideways.

High, low, etc.

"How many ways can you jump from here to here?"

Indicate tape marks or lines on the trampoline.

See above jumps plus: zig-zag, hop, turning, etc.

"How many ways can you hold (or move) your arms and jump?"

Up, out, one up and one down, windmill, etc.

"How many ways can you hold your head and jump?"

Chin tucked down, head turned, eyes straight up.

"What body parts can you touch while jumping?"

Back, shoulders, right heel, etc.

"How many ways can you use the bean bag and jump?"
   Toss and catch, hold under chin, between ankles, knees, etc.
"How many ways can you use the rope and jump?"
   Spin, jump over, spin overhead, etc.

Variations: Play "Copy Cat" or "Match My Stunt": one child does an easy stunt, jump or sequence; other children try to imitate it. Play add-ons. (See Balance Add-Ons, p. 17, or Tactile Add-Ons, p. 225.)

128. / Trampoline Songs, Chants, Counts

For:

Motivating children to continue jumping; endurance.
Balance, eye and whole body coordination and strength, especially of the legs.
A different type of visual steering.
A sense of rhythm.

Age: All ages. These activities are especially suitable for beginning jumpers.

Materials: The trampoline.

Directions:
   1. The very first time a child explores a trampoline is not the time for counting; however, shortly after the child is able to jump continuously and/or as a warmup, the teacher may begin a gentle counting. If done in a quiet voice, this is relaxing to the child and takes his mind off any insecurities he may be feeling. I hasten to add that it is not wrong for a child to feel insecure on the trampoline; and somewhere along the line, we should acknowledge these feelings.

   As the child continues, a louder, slower count will encourage the child to bounce higher.

   Children enjoy being counted for; they bask in this form of personal attention, and self-confidence takes a big step up. Even if they do not fully understand the concept of fifty or sixty, etc., they *do* realize they've jumped many, many times.

   2. Singing, like counting, motivates the beginning jumper to continue jumping and to try a variety of jumping styles. It accentuates the rhythm of the jump and contributes a different dimension to the experience. Almost any song will do. "Skip to My Lou" is ideal because the teacher can change it to encourage different types of jumping, for example:

Trampoline Songs, Chants, Counts

"Hop, hop, hop to my Lou,
Hop, hop, hop to my Lou,
Hop, hop, hop to my Lou,
Hop to my Lou, my darling."

Other possibilities:

"Spin your arms . . . to my Lou;
Jump high . . . to my Lou;
Twist, twist . . . to my Lou;
Bounce and clap . . . to my Lou;
Feet apart . . . to my Lou,
Feet together . . . to my Lou;
Jumping Jacks . . . to my Lou;
March around . . . to my Lou."

3. Chants: Any and all jump-rope chants lend themselves well to the rhythm of the trampoline. Most libraries will have books of such chants. All have a strong easy rhythm, and many are filled with humor and/or with counting or alphabet rhymes. Here is one example:

"Ice cream soda with a cherry on top.
Tell me the initials of my soda pop!
A-B-C-D-E-F-G,
H-I-J-K-L-M-N-O-P;
Q-R-S-T-U-and V;
W-X and Y and Z."

All of these chants are excellent for clapping rhythms, too. While we want to encourage continuous jumping for endurance building, children should also have ample opportunities to rest between jumping sessions.

129. / Around the World

For:

Balance, agility, endurance and fitness, rhythmic coordination.
Beginning awareness of the coordinates of space by clock positions and/or by compass positions. (Children will not fully understand these concepts until about age eight or older. Nevertheless, the idea that space may be structured according to a plan is useful information.)
Visual steering of body.
Following precise directions and learning to give commands to one's body (bringing control of the body into conscious awareness).
Eye-hand and eye-foot coordination.

Age: Primary. Younger children can play an easy version of the game but will not be able to absorb the high-level space concepts involved.

Materials: The trampoline, a bean bag or ball; 3 × 5 card markers are helpful but not necessary.

Introductory comments: Learning clock and compass positions, like learning left and right, is a long drawn-out and complex process which requires many low-level and varied exposures to set the stage for eventual deep understanding.

Because children do not fully understand clock and compass concepts until a later age does not mean we cannot begin to expose them to these concepts on a limited basis. We must keep in mind, however, that we are working on an *awareness* of the concepts, not mastery of them. Children are "inherently" interested in clock and compass positions, and are not frustrated by this game *if* we allow them to take from it as they are able and do not ask for or expect correct answers.

Directions: "Pretend the trampoline is a giant compass. (Discuss compasses and hopefully, show child one.) Here is north. (Teacher stands beside trampoline at north position; and child, on the trampoline faces north.) Bounce in that position. Directly opposite is south. (Teacher stands by south position.) Bounce facing south." Gradually add east and west, and if possible, mark the positions with a

Around The World

card and masking tape label. Move around the various positions while tossing and catching a bean bag or ball.

The same routine can be used for jumping the positions of the hours or minutes of the clock.

Advanced children could do a Simon Says game of Jump-the-compass positions, (or Jump-the-clock-positions) "Simon Says jump facing east, west, etc.," preferably with north, south, east and west clearly marked, until the child is very secure in his directions.

See also other Simon Says games, p. 188, which may be adapted to the trampoline.

34.

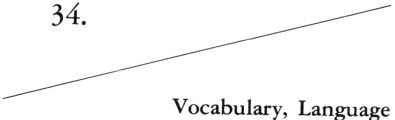

Vocabulary, Language and Speech Development

A child attaches meaning to words as she has active experiences with the objects, motions, or persons for which the words stand.

Perceptual motor games go with language like peaches go with cream. Though we sometimes think of movement games as purely physical, i.e., silent, they most definitely are not. One cannot play them without an abundance of receptive and/or expressive language. The beauty of the games is that "real," concrete sensory or motor experiences are instantly tied to matching language.

Keep in mind that *understanding* a word always comes long before the child *spontaneously speaks* a word. (Receptive language always precedes expressive language.) Therefore, it is much more difficult for a child to "think up and say" her *own* verbal expression than to understand or to imitate a verbal expression from the teacher.

130. / Language-Loaded Favorites

There is not a single game in this book that is not accompanied by the liberal use of language, including some language that will be new to the child.

Can any teacher afford *not* to have a regular perceptual motor game time of at least fifteen minutes a day? Please teachers, don't say, "I don't have time, there is so much real work to be done." Perceptual motor play *is* a child's real work.

Some of the very best language games are those that involve a series of changes (i.e., obstacle course or station-to-station games). Other universally rich

Language-Loaded Favorites

language sources are finger games and/or act-out songs, where words signal a simultaneous motion. Saying and doing are matched. In such games, there is what may be called comparative feedback, with many verbal and non-verbal experiences following in quick succession. One can almost see mental wheels turning and lights flashing. Some especially good games for language development follow, but the list is by no means exhaustive.

Blind Person's Carnival. (See Balance Games, p. 17.)

Bean Bag Activities. (See Object Handling, p. 125.)

Boards and Trestles (and other free play activities, especially when language is stimulated by the teacher).

Teacher Facilitated Dramatic Play (and other creative and imaginative play).

Improvised Obstacle Courses. (See Obstacle Courses, p. 134.)

Busy Bee (and all Body Awareness games, p. 30).

Rope Shapes I. (See Shape and Form Recognition, p. 182.)

Slap, Clap, Snap (and other finger games, singing games and rhythmics).

Rope Shapes II. (See Space Exploration, p. 209.)

Simon Says Games, p. 188.

How Many Ways? (See Trampoline Activities, p. 229.)

Touch By Ten. (See Tactile Games, p. 224.)

Spacewalk. (See Listening Games, p. 107.)

Seeing, feeling, hearing, thinking, moving and gradually speaking are so closely interwoven that in early childhood, they almost become one. By emphasizing any of these learning components, we enrich all the others.

It is helpful to remember that in the very early years, language learning (almost) never takes place without movement.

Appendix 1

Classroom Management Techniques

1. Schedule a regular perceptual-motor or "game time" preferably every day for twenty to thirty minutes. This should not take the place of free time, physical education or recess.

2. Never attempt a perceptual-motor lesson without having a briefly written (and therefore organized) plan. Knowing exactly what you are going to do decreases disciplinary problems and increases learning benefits; paradoxically, a well-laid plan facilitates appropriate departure from the plan. (See Question and Answer #6 and #7.) A firm plan enables a teacher to convey calmness and security to distractible children.

3. While a mastery of theory is not mandatory in starting a perceptual-motor program, a gradually increasing understanding of the "why's" as well as the "how's" of learning games adds immeasurably to the teacher's enjoyment and ease in this important area of childhood education. (See Question and Answer #2.)

4. Develop the habit of looking for and commenting on children's effort rather than achievement; positive reinforcement of even minimal moves toward your goals forestalls discouragement and increases children's involvement. Empty compliments are *not* what we are after; these soon become tiresome to children. Honest comment on what children are doing right, however, provides vital learning feedback and contributes to our children's information storage banks. (See Question and Asnwer #9.)

5. While fun, per se, is decidedly not our goal, it is one indication that the teacher's planning is hitting "on target." If children are not having fun in the game, something is wrong and they are letting us know it. Children uncannily respond with involvement and joy to games that are at their appropriate developmental level. (See Question and Answer #4.)

6. Misbehavior may be thought of as a child's only way of indicating that he or she is uncomfortable, frustrated or bored in the game. Simplifying a game, breaking it into manageable segments, or otherwise re-casting it so that it is more appropriate to the child's or class's abilities often remedies the situation. (See Question and Answer #6.)

7. Competition, if misused, can be a most destructive force that hurts both winners and losers. If used with great restraint, a touch of competition can add delight and interest to an otherwise routine activity. (See Question and Answer #5.)

8. Social give and take, courtesy and sportsmanship can and should be taught, directly and indirectly. Tell children *specifically how* they can show consideration to themselves and their classmates. A teacher who notices every child's physical and social efforts, no matter how clumsy, has gone a long way in demonstrating consideration and acceptance. The teacher should provide social skills instruction frequently. Still, a light and humorous touch (as opposed to a moralistic one) is much to be preferred.

9. Perceptual-motor games provide an ideal setting for the learning of language. Children may not only be introduced to many new words, but these words may become fixed in their minds through the actions which accompany them. Use new terms (and directions) freely, but make sure you explain them on the child's level.

10. Whenever feasible, tie new experiences (new games) to old experiences through brief teacher-child exchange of comments, experiences and/or little stories. Such meaningful "patter" before and after a game, and occasionally during the game, constitutes a vital learning resource. Such discussion usually must be carefully directed by the teacher to prevent rambling and to give quiet children opportunities to contribute.

11. Supplement clear verbal instructions with visual markers whenever possible; a string line makes "from here to over there" much more understandable. Standing on a tape or chalk mark, or on a rope circle, is much more helpful to a child than "stand in a line" or "space yourselves evenly in a large circle." Seeing a sketch of a bear or snake is an unmistakable signal that it's time to do the bear walk or snake crawl.

12. Give help as needed so that *every* child can be ninety percent successful in the games. Developmental planning (matching the type of game and standards of performance to children's ages, abilities and needs) largely assures that success is built in. In addition, the teacher should provide physical and verbal support to any child who is floundering. Physical help should be unobtrusively withdrawn at the earliest moment the child can do for himself

or herself. Verbal propping-up may gradually be tapered off and replaced with positive reinforcement of the child's independent thinking.

Questions Teachers Ask

1. *Developmental planning minimizes discipline problems and increases learning.*

   Question: Try as I may, I cannot tell ahead of time how my children will react to a new game. Sometimes they are enchanted; other times they fall apart and behave miserably. How can I avoid these chaotic situations, which are bad for me as teacher, as well as for the class?

   Answer: There is no absolute security in a teacher's life. However, there are several major ideas which can help insure that the learning game time will be profitably, if not richly, spent and that both teacher and class will have an orderly and pleasant experience. In order of value, the major helps to the teacher are (1) the developmental approach, (2) a carefully thought out and *written* plan, and (3) positive reinforcement of children's efforts.

   The developmental approach merely means selecting games that your class needs, that are at their level or slightly above, and that the class can succeed in. How does one decide what the class needs *are?* How does one decide what their level *is?* How can all children succeed without some children becoming bored? The teacher can consult a developmental chart (Appendix 2) to find out what four-year-olds, five-year-olds, etc. typically can and cannot do and what the sequence of motor skills is. From here, she can write out a series of simple goals, both long term and short term. With goals clearly in mind, it is not too difficult to plan an appropriate lesson. No matter what the lesson, no matter what games are chosen, the teacher will find that each child must participate at a level consistent with his or her abilities. Practically all the activities described in this book can accommodate a range of skills. The games may not only be easily adapted age-wise from class to class; they may be adapted to the varying abilities within any single class.

   Selecting games at the approximate developmental level of the class is the single most useful tool a teacher can have, and this approach will prove to be his or her greatest friend. Discipline problems will diminish, as children "by nature" want to learn and are built to seek the next higher learning stage with enthusiasm and confidence—providing that the next step is within their immediate reach. Selecting games at their appropriate developmental level helps insure interest, cooperation and maximum success. By planning developmentally, the teacher will save much time in the long run and acquire maximum educational benefits for the class.

2. *The difficulty of writing out long-term and short-term goals.*

Question: I am embarrassed to say this, but I am totally inept and unable to prepare educational goals in the perceptual-motor area. Would I be better off to drop all perceptual-motor activities from my curriculum?

Answer: Many teachers feel like fish out of water when it comes to writing perceptual-motor goals. As a temporary resort, I urge them to use a trial-and-error or cafeteria sampling approach, and to keep reading at least a little into perceptual-motor theory (and goal planning) whenever possible. To put the matter another way, the best approach is to have your goals in mind, then to pick games that develop these goals. But it is possible to learn to write goals via the back-door method: use the games first and from familiarity with what the games can do for your children, you will learn to establish goals and to develop a rationale.

Keep in mind that the words "theory," "rationale," and "goals" sound forbidding. In practice, however, even a *little* theory makes perceptual-motor work much more enjoyable for the teacher. It is satisfying to know the "why" of even simple childhood games.

The broad, major goals of perceptual-motor training will not differ greatly from class to class, nor even from year to year. The *level* of training, the quality and quantity of learning *will* differ according to age and ability.

We want to plan for growth and enrichment of all children according to the following list:

The Basic Six Perceptual-Motor Areas

1) Overall body strength and endurance.
2) Balance and coordination.
3) Space relations and space judging.
4) Eye movements and eye-hand coordination.
5) Sensory-motor integration.
    a. The ability to receive information (or perceive stimuli) visually, auditorily, tactilely and kinesthetically.

        b. The ability to integrate (organize, make connections) new with old information.

        c. The ability to mobilize an appropriate response, whether expressed in speech, gesture, action or writing.

    6) Self-awareness and self-confidence in a wide variety of learning (including social) situations.

It is obviously impossible to include work on all areas every day; however, our lesson plans should hopefully include work in all the above areas in a period of one or two weeks.

    There is an analogy between good perceptual-motor planning and good nutritional planning. In both cases, there are certain basic needs that must be met repeatedly. The vitamins, proteins and minerals of perceptual-motor skills are the goals (areas) listed above. The ways in which these needs will be met (games and activities) are many and varied, and the quantity of teaching (feeding) required to meet each child's basic requirements will differ slightly from individual to individual. In a rich and varied perceptual-motor program, the various children of a class may respond in differing degrees to our broad range of game "nutrients." Regardless, all will have basic needs met, and all will progress in health. As in nutrition, we do not expect to accomplish sweeping changes in any or all areas overnight, any more than we expect children to grow up overnight.

3. *Beginner's guide to writing daily and weekly lesson plans based on the Basic Six Perceptual-Motor Goals.*

    Question: Can you give an example of a comprehensive two-week lesson plan?

    Answer: Our perceptual-motor goals are broad, and progress is largely a slowly built, internal and often invisible operation; hence, it is difficult to measure. You can be sure, however, that progress is taking place. This does not mean that our planning need be haphazard. On the contrary, we must put extra effort into planning. Again, drawing an analogy to children's nutrition, modern parents and child care planners may start out by providing the Basic Four Food Groups. As they become more skillful, they will become increasingly precise as to the exact amounts of various nutrients needed, to varying age and/or individual requirements, and to increasingly skillful means of preparing and serving foods. Similarly for a young, inexperienced teacher or someone new to the perceptual-motor approach, it is possible to start a perceptual-motor program by meeting "the Basic Six" perceptual-motor goals in any one- (or two-) week period. (See Question and Answer #2.) As time goes on, hopefully the teacher will read in perceptual-motor theory and become increasingly discerning and specific in meeting both individual and group needs. The best way to master an understanding of perceptual-motor needs and teaching is to alternate 1) the reading of theory; and 2) testing it out in practice; 3) returning again into theory, and again trying it out. (See bibliography for appropriate sources.) Even a beginner (especially a beginner) should *never* attempt to conduct a perceptual-motor lesson on a given day without a written plan. This forces the teacher to organize his or her thinking and frees him or her to concentrate on the children and the game itself. For any given day, there should be perhaps two activities planned in detail, with a third ready in abeyance in case one of the original two does not work out.

A bi-weekly skeleton plan might look like this:

Major Goal (Objective)	Additional Benefits	Game	Materials Needed
Monday and Wednesday			
1. Overall body strength	Space judging; Eye-hand coordination	Selections from stunts and exercises	Mats
2. Space judging	Eye-hand coordination	Bean bag self-toss activities	1 Bean bag per child
(Extra game if needed)			
3. Space judging	Leg strength; Rhythmic coordination	Animal Tracks	Chalk or tape
Tuesday and Thursday			
1. Balance & coordination	Overall body strength and endurance; Visual steering	Trampoline activities	Trampoline
2. Tactile awareness	Body awareness; Relaxation	The Magic Feather	A large feather

(Extra games if needed)

3. Repeat any of Monday's activities

Friday			
1. Overall body strength and endurance	Body awareness; "Reading" visual signals (pictures)	Animal Walks	Four or five sketches of animal walks
2. Social skills: following a sequence of simple rules; catching and getting caught.	Space judgment	Frogs and Pollywogs	Chairs
(Extra games if needed)			
3. Arm, hand and finger coordination	Rhythmic sense	Rope spinning	Rope

Monday and Wednesday			
1. Balance-Coordination	Verbal planning; Body awareness	Blind Person's Carnival	2 Boards, 3 trestles
2. Eye-Hand coordination	Small space judgment; Visual-auditory-motor integration	Simon's Race-track	Chalkboard & chalk
(Extra game if needed)			
3. Sequential memory	Rhythmic finger coordination	Little Cabin in the Woods	Chalkboard sketches

Tuesday and Thursday			
1. Fine motor coordination	Listening skills; Quick thinking; Rhythmic sense	Slap-clap-snap	None
2. Agility and leg strength	Balance and co-ordination Space-time relationships	Jump the Shot	Rope and tetherball (or substitute)
(Extra game if needed)			
3. Listening skills	Translating auditory stimulus to words and/or gestures	What is Knocking At My Door?	A few objects that make noise

Friday
Repeat last Friday's
  lesson and/or any
  recent game that needs
  further practice.

---

4. *Fun vs. work*

   Question: You imply that game time should be fun, yet it is also serious work. I'm confused. Is it work or play?

   Answer: A game by definition is playful. A child's play is his work, and the lines between work and play are and should be almost nonexistent. Intense involvement and enjoyment, both for the teacher and the class, are highly desirable. If the teacher is involved and likes the game, usually the children will too.

   The enjoyment factor increases dramatically if the teacher knows the game thoroughly and knows exactly what to do next. Hence, a detailed, written lesson plan is always a great help to the teacher in organizing his or her thinking.

   Enjoyment must not be confused with silliness, which ruins a classroom game. Whimsy and humor—yes; slapstick—absolutely no.

   Children usually have more fun if the noise level is low. Paradoxically, during many of the best games children may *not* be laughing or even smiling. They are intent on the game and have quite a serious, rapt expression. Please do not misunderstand: smiles and laughter are not forbidden; the teacher must learn to differentiate between fun and clowning, the latter being definitely out of place during a learning game. In summary, a game should be, must be, fun for maximum learning to occur.

5. *Competition, winning and losing.*

   Question: What do you mean by "everyone who plays the game wins"? If this means what I think it does, won't it give children a false idea that they are achieving more than they really are?

   Answer: In nearly every learning game, every child learns something. In some games, each child learns a lot; at times the child learns little that is new but he may reinforce information partially assimilated into the learning bank. When either of these or related processes occur, the child is truly a winner. Children in a class should be told occasionally, even often, "what the game is good for," specifically what it teaches. This will not only *not* detract from the fun; it will enhance it.

Most children have a less than perfect self-concept and are all too ready to assume that if they are not in first or second place, they have accomplished nothing. Then too, in American culture, we have been taught that if someone is a winner in every game, we must also have losers. Teachers can help dispel these unfortunate notions first, by understanding in their own minds that every child does indeed win whenever he learns even a tiny increment of information or improves the slightest bit in coordination; and second, by repeatedly conveying to children that every child who attempts the game benefits from it.

6. *Learning to adapt a game and make adjustments on the spot.*

   Question: Sometimes I carefully prepare what I think is a delightful game, but it all falls apart in practice. What am I doing wrong?

   Answer: You may be doing absolutely nothing "wrong." Sometimes, even often, in spite of your best preparations a new game will flop. It may be too difficult or too easy, or something unforeseen causes it to fail. After some practice, you will learn how to adjust and recast a game on the spot: change the rules, add parts, slow it down, or speed things up. When these don't work, move to a new activity as gracefully as possible. Don't scold or apologize.

   Don't drop a game from your repertoire because it did not go well the first time through; rack your brain to analyze what went wrong. Very often a game which proved too difficult needs to be divided into component parts, each of which may be practiced separately before putting it all together into a game. Sometimes cumbersome rules can be simplified or eliminated. Sometimes just a slight dash of competition can change a "no-where" activity into a favorite.

   Next to always having a detailed, developmentally based lesson plan; the most helpful bit of practical advice might be: always plan more perceptual-motor activities than you expect to use. This provides backup material in case of an unforeseen eventuality.

7. *Structured games vs. free play.*

   Question: Do you really mean that all games must be planned and structured down to the last detail? Don't children need opportunities to fool around with game equipment using it *their* way, making changes in the rules, or even better, playing without any rules whatsoever?

Answer: The answer to both questions is "yes." There are many ways for teachers to teach games and many ways for children to learn from games. Let's talk about the teaching aspect first. Every teacher has a different style; some get good results with tight structure, others with a looser, non-directive approach. Likewise, children may learn some things best through a structured lesson and other things through undirected exploration and free play. The issue is complicated by the fact that most teachers use a combination of styles and most children need to learn by some combination of methods.

Given the many demands on a teacher's time, the urgent needs of most children to get specific learning messages from perceptual-motor games, and also the range of perceptual-motor abilities in any classroom, the writer strongly favors a regularly scheduled perceptual-motor or game time daily if possible, even if it is only fifteen minutes. Twenty or thirty minutes would be better. This should not replace physical education, particularly from kindergarten age up.

It is therefore important for the teacher to provide a rather formally scheduled game time, during which it is most efficient (if not absolutely essential) for the teacher to present directions explicitly, and for children to follow these directions quite precisely (insofar as they are able, of course). Most perceptual-motor games, by definition, follow a rather precise sequence; children need practice following this prescribed sequence and trying out all the steps, not just the ones that they might choose. Perceptual-motor game time is the time when children learn some rather precise skills in rather prescribed ways. Free play, creative activities and discovery games also have a definite place in the child's day. Children *must* have time to improvise, change rules, "mess around" and discover on their own, and this time should be provided without fail by additional scheduling. The point is that the two times (structured game time and free play) probably should not be mixed.

8. *Careful planning vs. the possible dangers of over-directiveness.*
   Question: Can a teacher be so well organized and precise in giving instructions that all the fun and initiative goes out of the game, and it

becomes an exercise in following orders? Won't an emphasis on structure be misinterpreted by some teachers as an excuse for top-sergeant, I-know-what's-good-for-you tactics?

Answer: Of course it's certainly possible to be overdemanding and nit-picky. Generally speaking, however, the better prepared a teacher is, the more both teacher and children can relax about directions and get on with the fun and the learning message in the game. For every game that might be spoiled by overcontrol, there are several that are spoiled by inadequate pre-planning. True flexibility comes from a secure knowledge of what one is about and *why*.

It should be emphasized that detailed pre-planning and firm structure do *not* preclude flexibility; on the contrary, they facilitate *appropriate* changing of rules, while enabling the teacher to hold firm in the face of children's whims.

9. *Setting standards of performance for the poorly motivated child.*

Question: How does a teacher know when to insist on a better try, when to ignore a rather poor performance and when to reinforce with praise?

Answer: The teacher's intuition is certainly not perfect, but it's surprisingly often a dependable guide. If you suspect a child can do better than he's doing, try to encourage him, even lure him, into trying the task again. The lure should be positive, as "You've almost got it." Or, to a child who doesn't want to use his weak left arm, you might say, "Your left arm doesn't want to be left out of the fun. Give Mr. Lefty a chance to play too." To a child who is afraid to disturb his fragile sense of balance and doesn't want to bend to either right or left, you might say, "Pretend you're a tree blowing in the wind—the wind is blowing harder and harder, etc." In other words, appeal when possible to the child's imagination. Sometimes when a child will not be lured, a simple statement as "It's time to go across the balance beam" will have a good effect. Children do not always have to be cajoled. Of course, the best motivator of all is to select appealing, even exciting, games which (again) are at the child's developmental level.

With all children, and especially the difficult ones, positive and honest comment on any small effort or tiny success is more helpful generally than all other disciplinary techniques combined. (See also Question and Answer #10.)

When you feel a child is deliberately doing a poor job, perhaps as a way of getting the teacher's attention, it often helps to ignore the poor behavior, and (1) wait for some small indication of positive behavior and comment on that: "Good watching, Sandy"; or (2) ignore the child's poor behavior and comment positively on other children who are exhibiting the desired behavior: "I like the way Jean and Brian and Billy are listening for the signal."

As a last resort, a child who is really unable to function may sit in a resting chair and watch until he can participate reasonably well.

On rare occasions, a child who is utterly unable to participate in perceptual-motor games without becoming overstimulated and going to pieces should be excused from game time for a few days or a few weeks and given another pleasant and profitable activity. The idea is not punishment, but a holding operation until the child becomes ready for the minimum self-control that is needed in active group games. Ideally such a child should receive individual perceptual-motor work, but this is not always possible.

Every attempt should be made to reintegrate such a child into the group as soon as he or she is ready as this is often the very child who most desperately needs perceptual-motor skills.

10. *Handling children's fears.*

Question: How should one deal with a child who is truly fearful (for example, of heights)?

Answer: Teachers will differ in the ways they can help children overcome fears. Answers will vary from ignoring fears and reinforcing any small attempt to overcome them; to gentle insistence; to seeking professional help for extremely fearful children. Of course, it is always best never to force. For example, if a child is truly fearful of walking a raised balance beam without support and it takes all his courage to stand alone at one end, it would be best that the teacher *not* insist that he walk the beam alone, even if the teacher was very sure the child could do it. A guiding motto might be, "Give all the help that's needed, but withdraw the help as soon as the child can do for himself. Reinforce positive action on the part of the child."

When the child overcomes some hesitancy and tries a new, perhaps frightening activity, even though that performance is really sloppy, it is strategic to ignore the errors and to reinforce every minute good thing in that performance. "You got across all by yourself. You used your arms to help yourself balance. You were very careful where you put your feet, etc."

11. *Parent-child perceptual-motor home supplementation.*

     Question: Should parents also be as directive in perceptual-motor work as classroom teachers?

     Answer: Structured, yes; directive, probably no. A command method would probably sour the parent-child relationship in a hurry. It is good to have a detailed plan in mind, but parents are not under the same type of efficiency-time pressure as the teacher in a large classroom. The parent is in the uniquely favorable position of being able to tailor the pace of the game to the child's needs, taking time as needed to repeat, to skip steps, to visit and to discuss as the parent and child wish. Only if the parent is doing specific remediation under a professional's guidance (as physical therapy) should the parent insist on the following of exact orders. Parent and child perceptual-motor games can be highly educational but should always be kept low-key, unpressured, and relaxed. If the parent and child are not enjoying the game and each other, there is probably little learning taking place.

12. *The use of "the story line" in motivating the class.*

     Question: Besides developmental selection of games and positive reinforcement, can you suggest any method for motivating and holding the attention of the little "negatives" in my classroom? There are one or two who almost always seem tuned out or turned off even before I announce the name of the game.

     Answer: If this sounds familiar, teachers, you are normal. This is such a common yet frustrating situation. Teachers often say, "I have a child in my class who daydreams during the directions. No wonder he is lost when it comes time to do the game; if only they'd listen—if only they'd try!" or "I wish I had a magic wand I could wave over my class to insure their attention at the start."

          What we teachers wouldn't give for an answer to some of these knotty and all-too-familiar problems. Is there an answer? Not a wand, not a magic pill, but there *is* a startlingly simple and readily available technique that usually grabs the attention and imagination of whole classes, even the poor listeners, and often transforms ordinary teachers into pied pipers and children into eager listeners and learners. It is what might be called "the story line."

Best of all, "the story line" is not a deceptive or empty gimmick. It is a living demonstration of the commandment, "Thou shalt, whenever possible, enhance physical activity with language." To the children, it becomes a model for how to improvise creatively; it teaches how to make believe and demonstrates the important skill of using motor expression to act out and enhance an idea. Contrary to what most people think, making believe is not an inborn behavior. Many, many children, especially those with learning disabilities or those from any variety of deprived environment, may need to be taught specifically how to pretend. And teacher, your story line need not be clever, funny or even very imaginative. *Any* story, no matter how pedestrian it seems to the teacher, will delight your children.

The story line may be used in two important ways: (1) Before the active game starts, a story might be told about some aspect of the game, for example, the characters that will be acted out, or how the equipment was made. The story might be a true one, like how a farmer might catch fish in the river to stock his pond. (See Catching Fish, p. 95.) Children may be encouraged to add their own related experiences to the story or discussion. The pre-game story might be complete fantasy, for example, how some toys came to life one night. (See Nylon Stocking Racquets, p. 131.) The class might be told a short version of a well-known story like "The Billy Goats Gruff." (See the Trolls and the Kids, p. 107.) (2) Another very important use of the story line is to tell a story a little at a time and act it out as you go along, for example, Rocking Boat, p. 92; "Pretend we're rowing up the Amazon River (everyone rocks). Now it's time to get out and swim (everyone jumps overboard and crawls). Now let's pretend we catch some whales, etc. etc." Children should be encouraged to add their dialogue to the dramatic play. See also Train Stations, p. 103, Blind Person's Carnival, p. 22; The Dog and the Squirrel, p. 40; Creative and Imaginative Play, p. 49; Teacher Facilitated Dramatic Play, p. 55; etc.

In many games, story lines will both precede *and* accompany the play of the game. The younger or more distractible the children, the more difficult the game; or the more routine the activity, the more important becomes the teacher's task of motivation and the more useful becomes a story accompaniment.

As with the tactful use and withdrawal of physical help, the teacher should encourage children's independent language. The teacher's story should serve as a *stimulant* to activity and language only, and should not dominate the entire game.

Appendix 2

Developmental Milestones

How to Use a Developmental Chart

There are at least four major benefits accompanying the use of a developmental perceptual-motor chart: (1) it may be a reassurance that a given child is developing normally; (2) it may be used as one clue to present or future difficulties in learning; (3) it may be used as a preliminary screening test in appraising the motor skills of a class; and (4) it tells you where a given class or child is, motorically. Once you have this information, it is not too difficult to find appropriate activities with which to proceed with a perceptual-motor program.
Examples:

    (1) George J. has taught a primary class for eight years now and is considered to be a creative, knowledgeable and experienced hand. He is able to cope with a wide variety of children's problems in imaginative and constructive ways.

        This year, however, something seems to be wrong. There are daily disciplinary crises, a general low frustration tolerance in the class and difficulties in learning simple classroom games. The truth is, the class in general seems not to be progressing the way he expects. George wonders, "Am I losing my touch?" By doing some informal screening based on a developmental chart, George finds a disproportionate number of children with perceptual-motor lags. This is the first clue that more extensive screening in all learning areas is in order. Those children with suspected problems then can be tested in depth.

    (2) Mary and Henry T. are a conscientious young couple who want to be the perfect parents of a perfect child. They eye every neighbor child nervously and mentally compare how quickly their daughter is acquiring

the usual childhood motor patterns. They are determined that their child must get off to a good start. If little Laurie does not do *all* the things the neighbors' children do, Henry and Mary wonder where they have failed. Indeed, Laurie seems to be getting whiney and tense, presenting the very symptoms the parents most fear. A developmental chart which indicates the broad range of normal motor growth is the first step in putting both parents and child at ease, so they may enjoy their relationship with their daughter without worry.

(3) Martha G. must work long hours at a low-paying job to support herself and her three children. She is a warm and devoted mother, but considers worrying over her child's motor skill development a luxury she cannot afford. "It's something you worry about with your first child only. After that you do better to throw away the book; children have always grown up somehow without checklists—in fact, they generally do better that way." The fact is her youngest child, Mark, has several perceptual-motor lags in development. Even in the way he walks, Mark sticks out like a sore thumb in his group at the day care center. The day care center is concerned, and Martha is annoyed with them. She feels the center simply is not doing its job well, and she is considering transferring Mark.

If these developmental lags could be corrected in the early years, Mark *may* have a better chance to grow up as a normal child without the frustrations and heartaches of impaired physical, mental or social functioning. A developmental checklist might convince the mother that further evaluation is needed; and it almost certainly will save this hard-pressed parent time and energy in the long run.

Common Questions Regarding the Use of a Developmental Chart

Question: Aren't there conflicts among developmental scales; that is, Source A says a child should skip by age four and a half; Source B says age five, and Source C says age six?

Answer: There is general, though not exact, agreement among the motor scales. A source of confusion for the reader arises because some scales present an *average age* (fifty percent of children pass) and some, particularly motor *tests*, present a *top age* (ninety percent of children pass). Ideally a chart should indicate a *range* of normal development: the top as well as the average acceptable age. (See the Denver Developmental Screening Test.) If a chart is confusing, try to find a better one or ask your school psychologist or pediatrician. Unfortunately, most charts cover preschool ages *or* elementary ages.

Question: Some charts are so vague I can't tell if my child is ahead of schedule, on schedule or behind schedule.

Answer: Don't use such a chart, or disregard confusing items. Some terms, like "builds with blocks," "dances to music," "attends," "cooperates" and "draws creatively" are so vague that they are meaningless.

    A good chart indicates a range of normal development, while also being specific enough to determine if the child passes or not.

Question: I am quite sure that my child is developing as a normal bright child should. Yet every time I apply a development scale, I start feeling uneasy. Don't these charts do a lot of harm in making parents and teachers uptight and discouraged?

Answer: You may not need to use a chart. A chart should always help and not discourage a parent or teacher.

    Misunderstandings sometimes arise as follows:

(a) The average age for balancing on one foot for ten seconds is four and a half years. To some readers this (erroneously) means that *every* child should be able to do this. In fact, the normal range for this skill extends from three to six years. Only fifty percent of the children tested have the ability to balance on one foot for ten seconds by age four and a half.

(b) Any single failure to meet a developmental standard is of little significance. If, however, there are several or many lags, further evaluation is in order.

(c) A developmental chart or scale should be used as a *rough* indicator of a child's development. If the parent or teacher still feels uneasy (while keeping in mind that no child is average in all ways), further evaluation of the child should be pursued.

Appendix 3

Composite Developmental Chart

Gross and Fine Perceptual-Motor Skills
90% of Children Will Have Acquired by Two Years of age

Gross Motor

Walks backward.
    (average age 15 months)
Walks upstairs with help.
    (average age 17 months)
Moves self from sitting to standing.
    (average age 18 months)
Seats self in small chair.
    (average age 18 months)
Uses rocking horse or rocking chair with
    aid.
    (average age 18 months)

Fine Motor

Builds tower of 2 cubes.
    (average age 15 months)
Builds tower of 3 or 4 cubes.
    (average age, 19 months)

Places pellet in bottle.
    (average age 15 months)

<u>Two Years (Fine Motor) (cont.)</u>

Places blocks in cup.
   (average age 15 months)
Places 4 rings on peg, or large pegs in pegboard.
   (average age 18 months)
Imitates vertical line stroke.
   (average age 20 months)
Turns pages of book, 2 or 3 at a time.
   (average age 21 months)

<u>By Two and One-Half Years</u>

<u>Gross Motor</u>

Kicks ball forward.
   (average age 20 months)
Jumps in place.
   (average age 23 months)
Runs (stiffly).
   (average age 2 years)
Hurls small ball overhand, 1 hand, without
   direction.
   (average age 22 months)

Pedals tricycle.
   (average age 2 years)

<u>Fine Motor</u>

Builds tower of 6 cube blocks.
   (average age 23 months)
Imitates circular motion with crayon, after
   demonstration.
   (average age 2 years)
Turns pages of book, 1 at a time.
   (average age 2 years)

By Three Years

Gross Motor

Walks up and down stairs without adult
help, but not alternating feet.
     (average age 22 months)
Walks 4 steps on tiptoe.
     (average age 2¼ years)
Jumps from bottom step.
     (average age 2 years)
Walks backward 10 feet.
     (average age 28 months)
Broad jumps 24-34 inches.
     (average age 2½ years)
Balances on 1 foot 1 second.
     (average age 2½ years)

Fine Motor

Imitates vertical line from demonstration.
     (average age 22 months)
Imitates vertical or horizontal line.
     (average age 2½ years)
Imitates V stroke from demonstration.
     (average age 2½ years)
Strings 4 beads in 2 minutes.
     (average age 2½ years)
Folds paper.
     (average age 2½ years)
Builds tower of 7 or 8 cubes.
     (average age 2¼ years)

By Three and One-Half Years

Gross Motor

Walks on tiptoe 10 feet.
> (average age 3 years)

Balances on one foot 5 seconds.
> (average age 3¼ years)

Fine Motor

Imitates bridge of 3 blocks from demonstration.
> (average age 3 years)

Copies circle from picture model.
> (average age 3 years)

Imitates cross from demonstration.
> (average age 3 years)

Closes fist, wiggles thumb.
> (average age 35 months)

Picks longer of 2 lines.
> (average age 3 years)

By Four Years

Gross Motor

Hops, preferred foot.
> (average age 3½ years)

Walks up stairs, 1 foot on each step, holding rail.
> (average age 3½ years)

Walks downstairs, 1 step per tread.
> (average age 3½ years)

Throws ball with direction.
> (average age 3½ years)

Balances on toes.
> (average age 3½ years)

Jumps over rope 8″ high.
> (average age 3½ years)

Swings on swing independently.
> (average age 3½ years)

Jumps from height of 12 inches.
> (average age 3½ years)

Holds standing balance, one foot advanced; eyes closed, 15 seconds.
> (one of two tries by 4 years)

By Four Years (cont.)

Fine Motor

Buttons up clothing.
(average age 3 years)
Cuts with scissors.
(average age 3¾ years)
Touches point of nose with eyes closed.
(by age 4, 2 of 3 tries)
Puts 20 coins in a box, separately.
(by age 4, 1 of 2 tries)

By Four and One-Half Years

Gross Motor

Balances standing on 1 foot, 5 seconds.
(average age 3¼ years)
Does forward somersault with aid.
(average age 3½ years)
Catches ball in arms, 2 of 3 tries.
(average age 4)
Catches bounced ball.
(average age 4 years)
Heel to toe walk.
(average age 3¾ years)
Jumps from height of 2½ feet.
(average age 4 years)

Fine Motor

Copies cross from picture model.
(average age 3¾ years)
Draws a man, 3 parts.
(average age 4 years)
Copies square from demonstration.
(average age 4)

By Five Years

Gross Motor

Balances on 1 foot for 10 seconds.
(average age 4½ years)
Hops on non-preferred foot.
(average age 4½ years)
Bounces ball 2 times successively with one
hand.
(average age 4½ years)

By Five Years (Gross Motor) (cont.)

Catches large bounced ball, 2 out of 3 tries.
     (average age 4 years)
Somersaults forward without aid.
     (average age 4¾ years)
Balances on tiptoes for 10 seconds; 1 out of
3 tries.
     (by age 5 years)
Jumps over cord at knee height, feet to-
gether.
     (1 of 3 tries)

Fine Motor

Draws man, 3 parts.
     (average age 4 years)
Builds pyramid of 6 blocks after demonstra-
tion.
     (average age 4½ years)
Clenches and bares teeth.
     (by age 5 years)

By Five and One-Half Years

Gross Motor

Walks heel to toe.
     (average age 3¾ years)
Walks heel to toe, backward.
     (average age 4¾ years)
Walks 2″ × 4″ balance beam, 3″ off floor,
without falling.
     (average age 4½ years)

Fine Motor

Draws diamond after demonstration.
     (average age 4½ years)
Copies square from picture model.
     (average age 4¾ years)
Ties a knot with lace; any knot that holds.
     (average age 5 years)

By Six Years

Gross Motor

Skips, both feet.
>   (average age 5 years)
Hops 5 yards, forward, either foot.
>   (by age 6*)
Two-handed catch of tennis ball, after
single bounce; 8 out of 10 tries.
>   (average age 5 years)
Balances standing on 1 foot, 10 seconds.
>   (average age 4½ years)

Fine Motor

Draws a man, 6 parts.
>   (average age 4¾ years)
Strings 8 beads in 25 seconds.
>   (by age 6*)

By Seven Years

Gross Motor

Balances on one foot 20 seconds, with arms
upraised.
>   (by age 7*)
Walks forward 10 steps heel to toe, keeping
balance.
>   (by age 7*)
Balances on tiptoes, bending forward from
hips.
>   (by age 7*)
Marches, skips to rhythm.
>   (average age 6½ years)

Fine Motor

Copies diamond from picture model.
>   (by age 7*)
Knows right and left on self.
>   (average age 6¼ years)

---

*Average age not available. Assume it is 6 to 9 months younger.

By Seven Years (Fine Motor) (cont.)

Can knit eyebrows (frown).
>   (by age 7*)

Sorts 36 playing cards into 4 piles in 30 seconds.
>   (by age 7*)

By Eight Years
Gross Motor

Jumps sideways, feet together, 3 successive jumps of about 12-14 inches.
>   (by age 8*)

Stork balance: Stands on one foot with sole of other foot against supporting knee, 20 seconds; 1 of 2 trials.
>   (by age 8*)

Crouches on tiptoes, 10 seconds; 1 of 3 trials.
>   (by age 8*)

Catches, on the fly, a tennis ball bouncing off a wall from a distance of 8 feet; underhand throw, two-handed catch; 4 out of 10 trials.
>   (by age 8*)

Fine Motor

Touches thumb to tip of all fingers of one hand, successively in 5 seconds; 1 of 2 tries.
>   (by age 8*)

Can wrinkle the forehead; lift eyebrows.
>   (by age 8*)

By Nine Years
Gross Motor

Jumps and claps twice before landing.
>   (by age 9*)

Balances standing on 1 foot, eyes closed.
>   (by age 9*)

*Average age not available. Assume it is 6 to 9 months younger.

By Nine Years (Gross Motor) (cont.)

Catches an underhand-thrown tennis ball,
one-handed, from distance of 8 feet; 6 of
10 trials, thrown by adult.
(by age 9*)
Jumps over rope 40 cm. high.
(by age 9*—boys, age 10—girls)

Fine Motor

Flexes and extends feet.
(by age 9*)

By Ten Years
Gross Motor

Balances on tiptoes, eyes closed 15 seconds.
(by age 10*)
Jumps and claps 3 times before landing.
(by age 10*)
Jumps, feet together, over rope at knee
height, lands on 1 foot, and balances 5
seconds; 1 out of 2 tries, each foot.
(by age 10*)

Fine Motor

Closes the eyes alternately.
(by age 10*)

---

*Average age not available. Assume it is 6 to 9 months younger.

Bibliography

Cratty, Bryant J., *Active Learning*, Prentice-Hall, Englewood Cliffs, N.J., 1971.

Frankenburg, William and Dodds, Josiah G., *Denver Developmental Screening Test*, University of Colorado Medical Center, 1969.

Frostig, Marianne, *Move, Grow, Lean* and *Teacher's Guide*, Follett Publishing Co., Chicago, Illinois, 1969.

Furth, Hans G., and Wachs, Harry, *Thinking Goes to School: Piaget's Theory in Practice*, Oxford University Press, New York, 1975.

Getman, G. N., Kane, Halgren and McKee, *Developing Learning Readiness*, Webster Division, McGraw-Hill Book Co., St. Louis, Mo., 1968.

Karlin, M., *Successful Methods for Teaching the Slow Learner*, Parker Publishing Co., Inc., West Nyack, N. Y., 1969.

Kephart, Newell C., *The Slow Learner in the Classroom*, Charles E. Merrill Publishing Co., Columbus, Ohio, 1971.

Kost, Mary Lu, *Success or Failure Begins in the Early School Years*, Chas. Thomas & Co., Springfield, Illinois, 1972.

Pangrazi, Robert P. and Dauer, Victor P., *Dynamic Physical Education for Elementary School Children*, Burgess Publishing Co., Minneapolis, Minn., 1975.

Radler, D. H., and Kephart, Newell C., *Success Through Play*, Harper & Row, N.Y., 1960.

Roach, E. G., and Kephart, Newell C., The Purdue Perceptual-Motor Survey, Chas. Merrill & Co., Columbus, Ohio, 1966.

INDEX